Fallingwater

Phaidon Press Ltd
2 Kensington Square
London W8 5EP

First published 1994

ISBN 0 7148 2995 1

A CIP catalogue record for this
book is available from the British
Library.

Library of Congress Cataloging
in Publication Data available.

Printed in Singapore

Fallingwater
Frank Lloyd Wright

Robert McCarter
ARCHITECTURE IN DETAIL

1

1 Frank Lloyd Wright, photograph taken during the period in
which Fallingwater was
designed and built.
2 Frederick Robie House,
Chicago, Illinois, 1909.
3 Taliesin, Frank Lloyd Wright's
own home and studio, built in
Spring Green, Wisconsin, 1911;
rebuilt 1915 and 1925.
4 Richard Lloyd Jones house,
Tulsa, Oklahoma, 1929,
perspective drawing.
5 Taliesin, stone walls and gate.
6 Edgar and Lillian Kaufmann
on the bedroom terrace at
Fallingwater in the 1940s.

Fallingwater, as Frank Lloyd Wright named the house he designed for Edgar and Lillian Kaufmann in 1935, is without question the most famous modern house in the world. Over 75,000 people visit the house every year, despite its remote site deep in the woods on Bear Run, a mountain stream in southwestern Pennsylvania, and it has been named the best American building of the last 125 years by the American Institute of Architects. While numerous books and articles have been written on Fallingwater, it has rarely been discussed as an experience, a place that we inhabit. Scholarly studies tend to search for new historical information rather than focusing on what is there for all visitors to see, if they only know what to look for; this text will attempt to break the prevailing silence about the spatial experience of Fallingwater, particularly of its interior. Constructive criticism is the result of a powerful, transformative experience, the quality of which we seek to communicate to others, hoping they will also feel compelled to undergo the same experience. As George Steiner said, 'In this attempt at persuasion originate the truest insights criticism can afford'.[1] This book is intended to encourage the desire to inhabit and experience this outstanding house by analyzing Wright's conception and development of the design, reviewing critical aspects of the construction process which brought the house into being, summarizing the exceptional qualities of the house by walking the reader through its site and its spaces, and briefly examining the importance of Fallingwater as a work of architecture.

The design of Fallingwater

In 1935, at the end of the Great Depression in America, Frank Lloyd Wright was already 68 years old. In the 43 years since starting his own practice in 1892, Wright had built hundreds of works, including the famous buildings of his Prairie Period such as the Robie House, the Martin House, the Dana House, the Coonley House, Unity Temple and the Larkin Building. He had left Chicago and its influential suburb, Oak Park, in 1911, retreating to the remote valley owned by his mother's relatives near Madison, Wisconsin, where he had built Taliesin, his home and studio. Here, at the age of 45, he had begun what many considered to be his second career with such works as the Midway Gardens, the Hollyhock House, the Imperial Hotel in Tokyo and the California concrete block houses for Millard, Ennis, Storer and Freeman, to name only the most famous. It was altogether a long and prodigious career by any reckoning, and one unmatched in America before or since. Wright's practice had all but disappeared in the economic decline of the late 1920s, his last built work being a house for his cousin Richard Lloyd Jones in 1929. He had written his autobiography during those slow years, summing up his seminal contributions to the development of an American architecture. So it should not be surprising that, by 1935, most people in America assumed that Wright had retired from practice, happy to bask in the glory of the new architectural histories that portrayed him as the grandfather of the modern architecture being built around the world. Joseph Connors notes that, given Wright's age, it seemed evident that, as these histories implied, 'he had pointed the way to the promised land that he would never himself enter'.[2]

2

3

4

5

It had never been wise to count Wright out, however; throughout his life he had repeatedly rebounded from a variety of personal and professional calamities, and was about to do so once again. As we might have guessed, given his extraordinary energy and creativity, Wright had not been idle during these years of professional inactivity; nor did he consider himself 'finished' as an architect. Even though he was then approaching 70, he would live to the age of 92, building hundreds of buildings in the next 25 years – his third career as an architect. Pivotal in this resurgence was Wright's marriage in 1928 to Oglivanna Lazovich, born in Montenegro and a follower of the Russian mystic Georgei Gurdjieff. When Wright founded the Taliesin Fellowship in 1932, offering apprenticeships to interested young students willing to work on the farm and in the drafting room, he to a large degree modelled this enterprise – with Oglivanna's guidance – on Gurdjieff's Institute in Fontainebleau; yet it was also related to Ashbee's Arts and Crafts colony near London, Hubbard's Roycrofters in East Aurora, as well as such American utopian experiments as Brook Farm, the Oneida Community, and New Harmony.[3] Opened in the very depths of the Great Depression, the Fellowship succeeded largely because of Wright's continued reputation as the greatest American architect; students enrolled from all over the country and the world, coming to Spring Green, Wisconsin, helping to rebuild the dilapidated buildings of Taliesin and the Hillside Home School, which Wright had built for his aunts in 1902, and which he now converted into the drafting room for the Taliesin Fellowship. The students received no pay for their work in construction, farming, cooking, cleaning and drafting at Taliesin – in fact, they paid Wright for the privilege.

One of the apprentices who joined the Fellowship in October 1934 was Edgar Kaufmann, Jr, a young art student whose father was Edgar Kaufmann, owner of the Kaufmann's Store in Pittsburgh. In 1871 the senior Kaufmann's father had been one of the founders of the Kaufmann's Store, a successful retail business offering ready-made men's clothing, which, by the time Edgar Kaufmann assumed control of the business in 1913, had become one of the largest department stores of its kind in the country. At the end of 1934, the Kaufmanns visited their son at Taliesin, and Wright was invited to Pittsburgh to discuss several projects, one of which was a country house to replace a rudimentary cottage that the family had used for over a decade; it was then that Wright first visited the site.[4] Bear Run, the stream over which the house is placed, was typical and unexceptional before it became the site for Fallingwater. Like many Appalachian mountain streams fed by springs in this area of Pennsylvania, it would never have attracted attention had it not been bought in 1933 by Edgar and Lillian Kaufmann as a site for their weekend house. In 1913, the year Kaufmann took over management of the family business, the store leased the Bear Run property for use by the employees as a summer and weekend camp; it had been similarly used since 1890 by the Masons, and there were 15 structures, including a clubhouse, a small train station, several cottages and a dance pavilion already existing on a 1,635 acre site.[5] In 1921, Kaufmann and his wife built a modest cabin on Bear Run, 1,500 feet southeast of the falls. With its screened sleeping porches

6

7 Wright and the Taliesin Fellowship apprentices, 1937. To the right are the two apprentices involved in overseeing construction of Fallingwater, Bob Mosher and Edgar Tafel; to the left of Mosher (with arms on desk) is William Wesley Peters, who developed the concrete cantilevered structural floors for Fallingwater.

8 Edgar Kaufmann's office at the Kaufmann's Store in Pittsburgh, designed by Wright.

9 Porter cottage and bridge existing on the Bear Run site prior to the construction of Fallingwater. The bridge is in the exact location of the bridge later built by Wright; the cottage occupies the site of the future guest house; and the main house would be located to the left, in front of the existing entry drive.

10 Fallingwater, view of the site before its construction, as seen from below the waterfall; photograph taken c1900.

11 Topographic site survey given to Wright by Edgar Kaufmann in March 1935. Note that the centre of the drawing – clearly intended by Kaufmann to be the building site for the house – is below and to the south of the waterfalls. Wright placed Fallingwater above and to the north of the falls, ensuring a southern orientation for the house.

7

8

9

and lack of plumbing, heating and electricity, it allowed the urbane Kaufmanns a true retreat from city life. The store employee's association bought the Bear Run property in 1926, with Kaufmann holding the mortgage; in 1933 the Kaufmanns assumed personal ownership of the original property, and were eventually to add to it until the property included 1,914 acres, enough to protect and conserve the watershed of Bear Run.

Wright returned to Taliesin and was sent a site survey in March of the following year, showing the stream, contours, major trees and boulders. Nine months went by after Wright's visit to the site with no discernable evidence that he was thinking of a design for the Kaufmann House; yet, in writing of his own design process a few years before, Wright had stated that one should 'conceive the building in the imagination, not on paper but in the mind, thoroughly – before touching paper. Let it live there – gradually taking more definite form before committing it to the draughting board. When the thing lives for you – start to plan it with tools. Not before ... It is best to cultivate the imagination to construct and complete the building before working on it with T-square and triangle'.[6] Not very helpful advice for most mortals, but it appears that Wright followed this method in his initial design for the Kaufmann House. Various apprentices have conflicting memories, but Bob Mosher and Edgar Tafel, both of whom would serve as on-site supervising apprentices during Fallingwater's construction, tell the same story of Wright receiving a call from Kaufmann one Sunday morning in late September, saying to Kaufmann, 'Come along, E J, we're ready for you'.[7] Kaufmann was leaving Milwaukee for Taliesin, a mere two-hour drive, and not a single drawing had been made! The understandable panic of the apprentices did not disturb Wright as he set about drawing first the three floor plans, working on top of the site survey and using different coloured pencils for each floor, next a north–south section through the house, and finally a south elevation from across the stream. Donald Hoffmann has written, 'His sketches may have looked a little rough to Kaufmann [who had no idea they had just been drawn], but they turned out to be a remarkably complete presentation of the house as it would be built: the house had been conceived with an awesome finality'.[8]

Kaufmann arrived, and was presented with the design, which he approved, despite its being in a different location on the site than he had apparently imagined. The area selected to be surveyed on the site map suggests that Kaufmann expected the house to be built to the south of the stream, looking at the falls from below.[9] Kaufmann was in fact surprised that the house was to be built above the falls, but Wright had no intention either of having the house face north, an inappropriate orientation for the sun, or to have the waterfall present merely as an image to be looked at from the house. He told Kaufmann, 'I want you to live with the waterfall, not just to look at it, but for it to become an integral part of your lives'.[10] Wright pointed out the critical difference between hearing the waterfall (an intimate, nearer experience) and simply looking at it (a formal, distant experience) when he later described the design, saying of Kaufmann, 'He loved the site where the house was built and liked to listen to the waterfall. So that was the prime motive of the design. I think you can hear the waterfall when you look at the design. At least it is there, and he lives intimately with the thing he loves'.[11]

In laying out these early sketch-plans, Wright had oriented the site map so that the existing roadway cutting across the face of the hill above the falls was horizontal, as was the waterfall itself; the house was laid out at a 60-degree angle to the road and falls. The three main concrete piers, which were the first things Wright drew, were set perpendicular to the stream, parallel to the existing bridge, so that the house faced 30 degrees east of due south. This provided for the dynamic diagonal views of the house both from the entry drive and from the flat rock ledge below the falls. As Connors put it: 'Thus if the house was photogenic it was not by accident. The picturesque view from the boulder downstream ... was built into the design from the start, and to make sure the visitor took it in, a set of stairs was cut into the riverbank leading down to the chosen viewpoint'.[12] These diagonal views were documented in a series of perspective drawings completed soon after Kaufmann's visit,[13] including the famous drawing

10

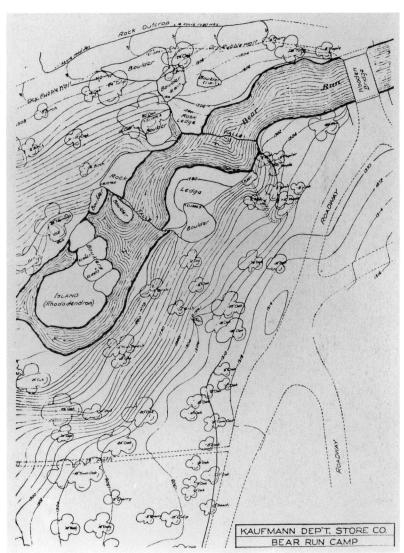

KAUFMANN DEP'T. STORE CO.
BEAR RUN CAMP

11

12 Fallingwater, sketch perspective, as seen from below the waterfall.
13 Fallingwater, sketch perspective from hillside across stream.
14 Fallingwater, final perspective rendering from below waterfall. This drawing appeared on the wall behind Wright in the cover photograph of *Time* magazine, 17 January 1938.

15 Samuel Freeman House, Los Angeles, California, 1923. Mitred glass corners with no vertical mullions.
16 Mrs Thomas Gale House, Chicago, Illinois, designed 1904, built 1909. 30 years later, Wright had trellises similar to those at Fallingwater added to this drawing (at the far left), and stated that this house was the 'progenitor as to general type' for Fallingwater.

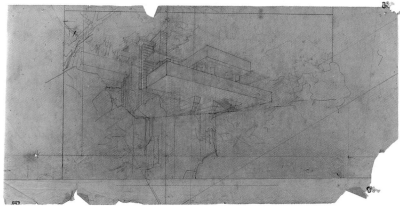

12

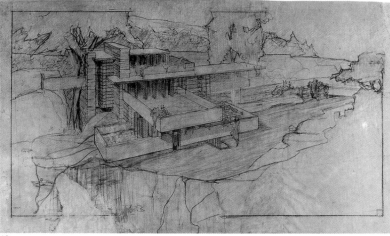

13

by Wright's own hand of the view from below the waterfall. This beautiful perspective, done with colour pencils, appeared in the background when Wright's photograph appeared on the cover of the January 17, 1938 issue of *Time* magazine, in which he was profiled and the house introduced to the country.

Historians have often claimed that the design for Fallingwater, with its smooth rectangular concrete planes interlocking and cantilevering out into space, was in some way Wright's 'answer' to the International Style of architecture that had been canonized in the 1932 Museum of Modern Art exhibition. But an examination of Wright's earlier work, and the close relation of Fallingwater to it, indicates this to be an invention on the part of the historians. Wright was quite specific about this, saying of Fallingwater: 'The ideas involved here are in no wise changed from those of early work. The materials and methods of construction come through them ... The effects you see in this house are not superficial effects, and are entirely consistent with the Prairie Houses of 1901–10'.[14] In briefly analyzing the sources for Fallingwater evident in Wright's own earlier work, we will find that the lack of preliminary sketch studies in his design process was possible due to the fact that he designed buildings in sequence, as variations on a common theme – spatial, constructional or site-specific. These sequential designs can be treated as the preliminary studies for Fallingwater, part of what Wright called the 'constantly accumulating residue of formula'[15] that he achieved by designing each building not as a single unique form but as part of the development of spatial types, perfected through a series of designs for different buildings.

Wright himself stated that the house for Mrs Thomas Gale, designed in 1904 and built in Oak Park in 1909, was the 'progenitor as to general type' for Fallingwater, and he had his apprentice John Howe add a roof trellis similar to those at Fallingwater to the original perspective for the Gale House, even though this detail did not exist on either the working drawings or the house as built.[16] Even without this detail, the Gale House develops a number of elements that would later be used in the design for Fallingwater. Despite having a simple rectangular plan, when seen from the front the house appears to be a series of horizontal planes and balconies projecting from a core of vertical slab-like walls, with only continuous window bands separating the horizontal elements. Finished in stucco plaster, its exterior has a similar texture to concrete, and, like Fallingwater, the Gale House is designed to take maximum advantage of a diagonal view. The primary cantilever of the balcony that runs along the stream at Fallingwater finds its precedent in the Frederick Robie House, built in Chicago in 1909; the enormous cantilever of the main roof is complemented by a series of crossing trajectories at second floor level and in the brick piers and walls below, and the whole is adjusted to attain the greatest impact in the diagonal perspective view from the street corner.[17] The rustic, beautifully-set stonework of Fallingwater was first employed by Wright in his own home, Taliesin, built in Spring Green in 1911, where he also contrasted it to the smooth golden plasterwork inside and out. The open glass corner, with the horizontal steel mullions passing around the corner and the vertical joint unframed, which runs up three storeys through the kitchen and small bedrooms at Fallingwater, was initially built out in the Samuel Freeman House of 1923 in Los Angeles, and later in the Richard Lloyd Jones House of Tulsa, Oklahoma in 1929. Fallingwater's balconies cantilevering all around from a central structural core are seen in the Malcolm Willey House project of 1932, and their structural interpretation in reinforced concrete appears earlier in projects for the Elizabeth Noble Apartment Building and the St Mark's Tower, both of 1929. Finally, despite its differing countenance on the exterior, the plan of Fallingwater was developed, as Wright said, from those of the Prairie Houses; the basic organization of a cruciform interpenetrating a square is to be found here, as is the typical asymmetrical, spiralling, perimeter movement pattern and hidden entry.[18]

The plan of Fallingwater, first emerging in the drawings done while Kaufmann made his way to Taliesin that Sunday morning, emphasizes the underlying order of the series of parallel walls and piers, standing on the rock ledge perpendicular to the stream on its north shore, which support the main volume of the house.

14

15

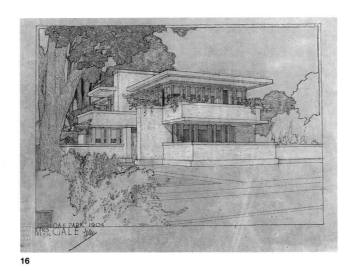

16

17

10

These are located on five equally-spaced lines that are struck across the drawing, creating four bays defining, starting from the east or entry side: the loggia and east terrace; the entry, library and stair down to the stream; and the living-dining room. A fifth equal bay, not defined by Wright in the same way as the others on any of the early drawings (by a line struck across the plan), defines the kitchen behind and the edge of the balcony overlooking the waterfall. In the main floor plan, the pier lying under the centre of the living room is not matched, as the others are, by a square stone pier or wall rising through the living room to support the floors above; only the dining table's central position marks this hidden support below. Though Wright's initial plan suggests that the house's 'centre of gravity' would be along the east edge of the living room, where the two stairs begin their ascent and descent, the two piers, fireplace and entry wall of the living room create a square central volume, off the corners of which open the entry, stairs, kitchen and balconies. This 'great room' contains in a single volume almost all the rooms – living, dining, library and entry – typically found in the first floor of Wright's Prairie Houses; only the kitchen remains outside. In those early houses, Wright's overall symmetrical order in plan allowed the corners to open; here the open corner becomes such a strong spatial element in its own right that it allows the plan to do without literal symmetry. The house is held together by the diagonal tensions between intimate internal places, so that the outer edges are free to respond to the natural site, as when the rear wall of the house steps along the drive in response to the natural rock wall of the hill behind.

The construction of Fallingwater

As with all of Wright's buildings, the designing did not stop at the start of construction. Of particular interest are Wright's many statements about how much he learned from the contractor and construction workers on his jobs, and how often this new knowledge allowed him to change and improve the design during construction. At other times he saw in the rising forms new spatial opportunities that had not been apparent during design even to his imaginative inner eye, requiring changes that included the removal and reconstruction of parts of the building already completed.[19] This necessitated Wright's regular presence on the construction site, which had been the rule during the earlier phases of his career. However, with the rapid nationwide expansion of his practice during the period of Fallingwater's construction – the Johnson Wax Buildings in Wisconsin, his own projects in Arizona, the campus for Florida Southern College, and the Usonian Houses being built from east to west coast – Wright relied more and more on his Taliesin apprentices to undertake construction supervision. While Wright had an astonishingly accurate intuitive sense of materials and their constructional and structural possibilities, he was often unable to pass this on to his apprentices; Wright's judgements made on the construction site were inevitably and unnervingly correct, but his dictates from afar were noticeably less so.[20] However, not following exactly the drawings done under Wright's supervision at Taliesin, or allowing the contractor to make changes not first specifically approved by Wright – even if they seemed clearly called for – would, if discov-

18

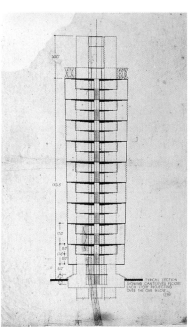

19

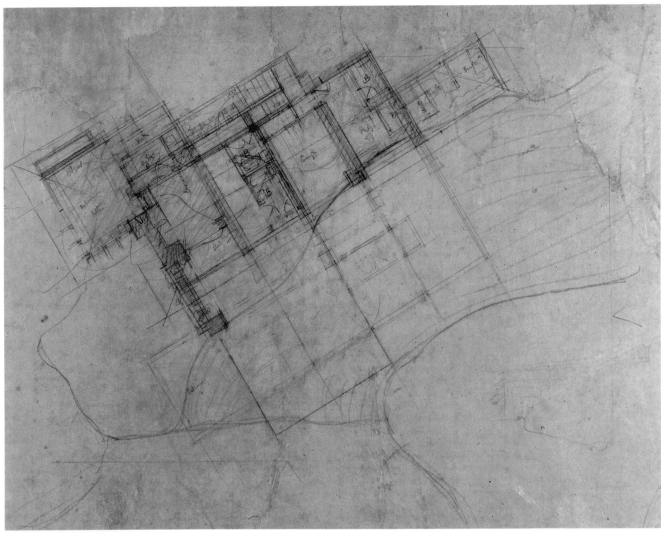

20

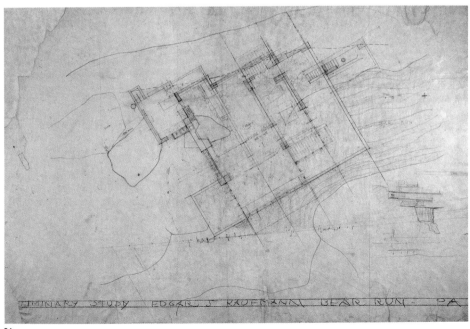

21

ered by Wright, result in the apprentice being recalled to Taliesin and replaced by another. Wright's apprentices were thus in a no-win situation when alone and facing a dilemma on the construction site, with predictable results.

Preliminary plans had been sent to Kaufmann on October 15, 1935, and after visiting the site again Wright told him to assume that the minimum cost for the house and its furnishings would be $35,000; he gave no maximum, and Fallingwater finally cost $75,000 for initial construction, $22,000 for completion and furnishing. The guest house, garage and servants' quarters added in 1939 cost an additional $50,000. Towards the end of 1935, an old rock quarry was opened about 500 feet west of the waterfall, and Kaufmann wrote to Wright that 'they are taking the strata of the stone as it comes and breaking it up in pieces about 12 inches to 14 inches wide and 24 inches long, the thickness being the strata of the quarry'.[21] Final plans followed in March, and Kaufmann reported that he was having a sample wall built; he did not tell Wright he was having the plans reviewed by his consulting engineers, who from the very start were doubtful about both Wright's competence with a material like reinforced concrete, still considered 'new' in America and untried in domestic construction, and Wright's decision to place the house on the rock ledge over the waterfall. The reviews were sent to Wright, who immediately told Kaufmann to return the drawings to Taliesin, 'since he did not deserve the house'. Kaufmann apologized and gave his approval for the working drawings – he later had the engineers' reports buried in the stone wall near the dining table.[22] Wright visited the site in April, approving the stonework in the sample wall, but in early June he rejected both the stonework and the concrete on the bridge, which had to be completely rebuilt. As the construction progressed, Kaufmann suggested a number of small but important changes and additions to the design, the first of which was the plunge pool to the north of the shallow stream, which had not been in the original plans. The Taliesin apprentice Bob Mosher was assigned by Wright to live on the site and supervise the construction, and in addition he sent Wright specific measurements to help with incorporating those of Kaufmann's proposals with which Wright agreed.

By the first week of August the formwork was being built for the concrete slab of the first floor with its extended cantilevers; Wright had ignored the engineers' recommendation that the pier-walls supporting this floor be three feet in width rather than two feet, as he had designed them. Wright had absolute confidence in his own structural intuition as well as that of his chief associates in this area: Mendel Glickman, an older structural engineer with the Fellowship, and William Wesley Peters, a brilliant, largely self-taught structural thinker who remained all his life with Wright at Taliesin. Peters and Glickman were responsible for calculating the structural loads in the revolutionary, thin-shell, reinforced concrete, hollow 'mushroom' columns that Wright sketched intuitively for the Johnson Wax Building in 1937, which held five times their design loads, and at Fallingwater they calculated the loads in the reinforced concrete, double-cantilevered slab with integral upturned beams that supported the flagstone floor – an upside-down early version of the 'waffle' slab capable of the 18 foot cantilevers out over the stream. This ingenious design placed the flat slab on the bottom, forming the ceiling of the space below; as the flagstone floor conceals from above the space inside this structural slab, only by studying the section drawing can we discern the integral beams that, with the balcony walls at the edge, do the real structural work in this floor.

The most serious mistake in the construction of Fallingwater was made by the contractor, engineer and Kaufmann in the pouring of this first floor slab on 19 August; at Kaufmann's request the engineers had redrawn Wright's reinforcing plan for the slab, and by their own admission, 'put in twice as much steel as was called for on [Wright's] plans'.[23] This excess steel not only added enormous weight to the carefully calculated slab, but was set so close together that the concrete often did not properly fill in between the reinforcing bars, causing an actual loss of strength. In building the wooden formwork to hold the concrete while it was setting, the contractor also neglected to build in a slight upward curve or 'camber', to compensate for the structurally insignificant and normal

22 Fallingwater, axonometric (redrawn) showing Wright's ingenious 'waffle' slab design. **23** Detail section and elevation of living room, looking east towards entry. Stone stairs going up at left, suspended stairs at 'hatch' going down to stream at right.

24 Preliminary section. Initial design indicates boulder at living room to be cut off flat, flush with floor.

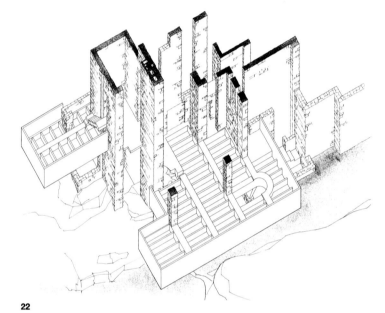

22

12

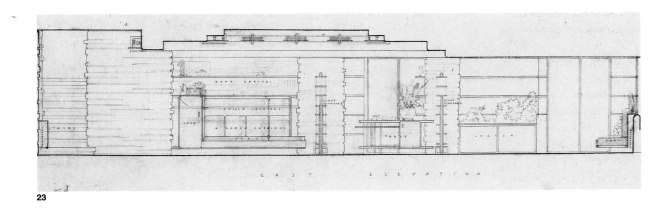

EAST ELEVATION

23

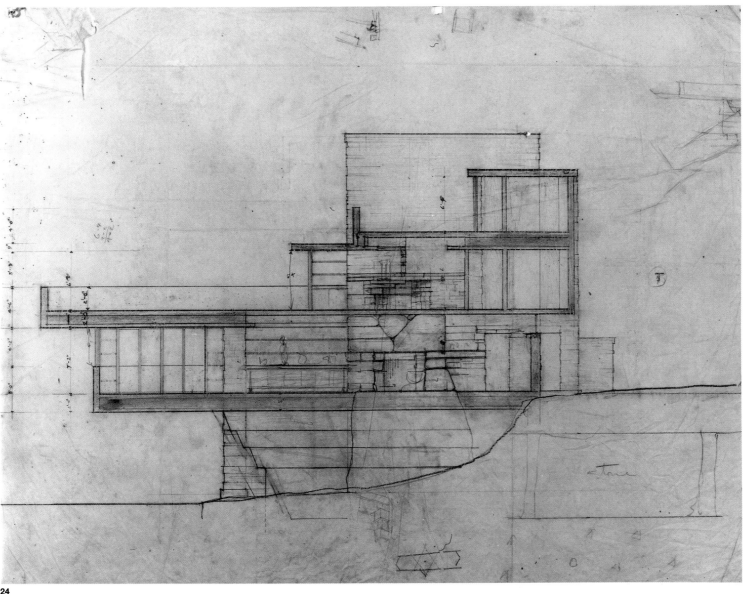

24

slight settling that occurs over time in reinforced concrete that spans or cantilevers. The result of these blunders, of which Wright was unaware at the time, are the drooping lines of the main cantilever and the cracks in the concrete that have plagued the house since its completion. That Wright's initial design, refined by Glickman and Peters, has been easily able to sustain these added structural loads and construction weaknesses, argues convincingly for the quality of their structural intuition. By early September, Wright found out about the extra steel in the first floor slab and called Mosher back to Taliesin in disgrace; Wright replaced him with the apprentice Edgar Tafel, but Mosher was later to return to Fallingwater.

Despite their complicity in the gravest error made during Fallingwater's construction, the consulting engineers continued to cast doubt upon the structural viability of the house even as construction proceeded. When Wright extended the west terrace out to 28 feet in length, the engineers recommended that a stone wall be added under the principal beam to reduce its span from 16 to eight feet. During the test-loading of this terrace, Wright discovered the added wall; 'No one had asked him about the wall, so he did not tell anyone when he ordered Mosher to take out the top course of stones', noted Hoffmann.[24] Kaufmann eventually told Wright about the wall, saying that if Wright had not noticed it, it must not detract from the house. Wright calmly took Kaufmann under the terrace, showing him the cantilever that had held up under test loads for over a month without the new wall's support; the wall was removed. Throughout the construction, Wright exhibited total disdain for those who doubted the structural integrity of the house; after the first floor slab was set, but while it was still heavily braced with wooden framing, Wright made a show of walking under the house, even kicking out some of the wooden supports.

In the design and construction of Fallingwater, Wright displayed acute sensitivity to the natural site, attempting wherever possible to save trees and retain rock outcroppings in their original form. There was less excavation and removal of rock in the building of the house itself than that which occurred in the small quarry that served as the source for its rock walls. The concrete trellis over the drive curves dramatically in two places in order to go around the trunks of trees close to the walls of the house. The cantilevered floor slab of the west terrace, with its three transverse beams anchored directly into the huge boulder next to the driveway, had three holes in the basic structure framed around existing trees to save them and allow them to grow right through the slab when completed. Wright's suggestion that the concrete be given a finish coat of gold leaf was rejected by Kaufmann on the grounds that it did not belong in what he termed his informal 'mountain lodge', saving Wright from one of his less appropriate ideas. What Wright was after for the colour of the concrete was something that would appear to be of the earth, and the house today exhibits a harmonious blend of grey stone, light golden painted concrete, and 'Cherokee red' painted steel mullions.

In this attempt to create a place in harmony with nature, the windows at the kitchen and small bedrooms, without vertical framing at the stone wall, allow inside and outside to merge in a way very similar to the flagstones which are set in the floor so that the joints seem to continue beneath the glass doors out onto the terraces. While historians maintain that Kaufmann suggested running the glass directly into the stone, and some have even described (incorrectly) the stone slot as having been cut with a saw, the pattern of the rock wall, with the slot carefully left between the differing stone patterns on either side, leads us to suspect that Wright conceived this detail well before construction. Perhaps the most telling instance of Kaufmann's contributing to the 'natural' feeling of the house came in the living room with the original boulder that, emerging from the flat slate floor, served as the hearth for the house; Wright had intended to cut the boulder off flat, even with the slate floor, but – much to Wright's delight – Kaufmann suggested it remain as it was when his family used to picnic upon it before the house was built. Here we can see, even during construction, that Wright was ready to incorporate ideas that would enhance the spatial and experiential richness of his designs.

14

25

26

The experience of Fallingwater from without

The natural beauty of the extensive site is what we first notice upon arriving at Fallingwater.[25] As we walk through the woods, we are not aware of the house ahead, for Fallingwater does not dominate its site as country houses have traditionally done, by being placed on the top of the highest point or at the end of a cleared axis. Here we are introduced to the character and natural features of the landscape during our winding approach, noticing the rock walls, exposed by weather and stream erosion, composed of thin horizontal layers of Pottsville sandstone, varying from dark grey to a lighter buff colour. Near the stream grows the flowering rhododendron, and there are white, black and red oaks, birch, tulip, maple, hickory, butternut, apple and wild black cherry trees near the waterfall.[26] In the summer the house can hardly be seen due to the denseness of the green vegetation; in the autumn the coloured leaves, complementing the light golden colour of the concrete terraces, add an element of beauty that is extraordinary; in the winter, with snow cloaking the flat roofs and terraces, the house appears to be an extension of the flat rock layers of the waterfall more than at any other season. The rock walls at Fallingwater are directly related to the rock cliffs in Wright's home country,[27] the rock walls of Taliesin that he built from that inspiration, and finally the rock walls of the stream of Bear Run. Visitors who detect the close resemblance between the natural rock walls of the stream and the walls of Fallingwater are often surprised to discover the close relationship with Wright's works in the Wisconsin hills.

When the house first comes into view, we are somewhat surprised to see across the stream from us a series of horizontal terraces that float without visible means of support. We had expected our first view of the house to be the famous perspective from below the falls, Wright's favourite drawing of the design, and one that has been published so widely as to become the iconic image of Wright's work. While that famous view may be easily attained by turning left and descending the rock-cut stairs (put in by Wright) to reach the large level boulder in the middle of the stream below the falls, the more reserved perspective with which Wright introduces the house is worth considering. In his perceptive analysis, Robert Harrison has noted that Fallingwater's 'fame as a masterpiece of architectural design seems strangely at odds with the feature for which it is famous, namely its discretion ... the fact that the house not only comes to rest in its environment but also embodies an extension of the foundation upon which it rests'.[28] In this house, Wright has created a powerful dichotomy; the natural rock layers are repeated almost exactly, in thickness and random pattern of setting, in the vertical walls that emerge from the boulders above the waterfall, while the lighter-coloured horizontal reinforced concrete terraces and roof planes exfoliate from this rock wall core, cantilevering both along and across the stream. This opposition between vertical/mass/earth and horizontal/floating/sky reflects the natural condition found in the trees, their roots and trunks anchored to the earth and their limbs and leaves cantilevering out into thin air. The stability of the house, its rooted condition, is unexpectedly emphasized and reinforced by the flow of water under it; rather than undermining the anchored quality of the house, Harrison notes how 'the dynamic relation between flowing water and solid foundations'[29] imparts to the house a sense of repose on the earth – it appears to have grown from its site. Wright said that 'it is in the nature of any organic building to grow from its site, come out of the ground into the light – the ground itself held always as a component basic part of the building itself'.[30]

Standing across the stream, we are made more aware by the house of the forces underlying this typical forest clearing; in building this house, Wright transforms this space that could be anywhere in the forest into a specific place, a place that is remembered. Wright said: 'We start with the ground ... In any and every case the character of the site is the beginning of the building that aspires to architecture ... All must begin there where they stand'.[31] The house crystallizes and gives form to the vertical and horizontal tensions latent in the waterfall itself, exaggerating and thus making evident the vertical stacking of the rock layers in the natural cliff walls and the cantilever of the rock slabs over which the water cascades; as Wright said, 'In the stony bonework of the earth, the princi-

25 Construction photograph, 1936. Wooden formwork under first and second floor concrete slabs.
26 Construction photograph, 1936. Second floor stone masonry walls; near centre shows a wall with slot for glass laid into masonry (not cut in later, as is often stated).
27 Construction photograph, late 1936. Reinforced concrete beam structure in bedroom terrace on west side of house. Existing trees are accommodated by openings framed into terrace floor; three major beams bear onto existing stone outcropping along driveway.
28 Construction photograph, autumn 1936. Wooden formwork under first floor concrete slab, removed from under second floor slab. The contractor's storage shed may be seen at the edge of uppermost level.

27

28

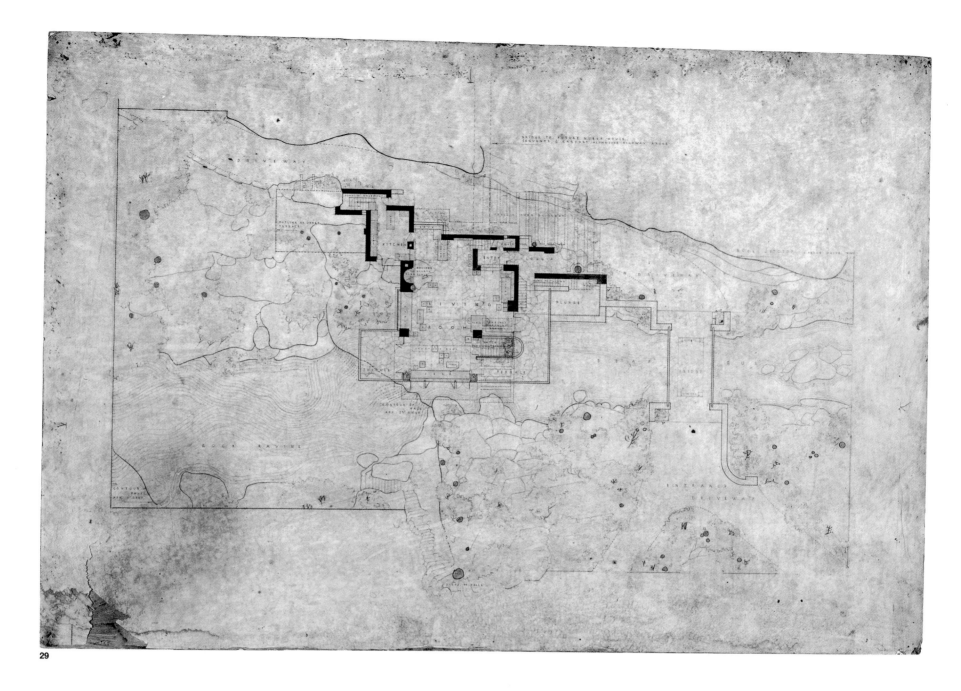

29

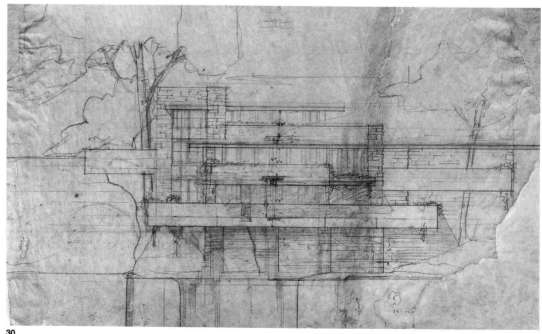

30

ples that shaped stone as it lies, or as it rises and remains to be sculpted by winds and tide – there sleep forms enough for all the ages, for all of man'.[32] What was a small and typical natural event along a stream becomes, with the construction of the house, a unique and habitable space where we are made far more aware of the waterfall and its natural surroundings than we could possibly have been before the house came to make this place. The house draws all the profiles of the landforms to itself, resolving them within its order; as Martin Heidegger said of a similar architectural and structural construction of landscape occupation and clarification, 'the bridge gathers the earth as landscape around the stream'.[33] The house-as-a-place brings the landscape into focus, into presence, to be experienced as part of human life. Only places where man has decided to dwell, can make the site fully present for us. Fallingwater does not stand on the site so much as it makes the site stand forth, 'building the site',[34] allowing it to come to our attention, to come into being as a human place, to become a place of memory.

The vertical rock walls make the house's actual anchorage to the ground, but the horizontal floating planes nevertheless still relate to the earth, in a larger sense. Wright said: 'I see this extended horizontal line as the true earth-line of human life, indicative of freedom. Always'.[35] Most important for Wright was the way in which the emphasis on the horizontal acted to ground the house, making it a true foundation for the life within; 'the horizontal planes in buildings, the planes parallel to the earth, identify themselves with the ground – make the building belong to the ground'.[36] In the forest, thick with trees and fractured by rock walls, Wright restates the horizontal as the datum of human dwelling, its freedom indicated by the way in which the horizontal concrete planes turn and interlock as they layer one above the other. As Harrison points out: 'the search for freedom in horizontality, and not in the celestial nostalgias of the vertical rise, makes of Wright an American in the exceptional, Thoreauvian sense. Whatever freedom we may call ours is to be found on the earth, whose surface is round only from a perspective beyond the earth. For those on the earth its surface extends horizontally, that is to say, constitutes a horizon. A house is that which gathers the horizon around itself'.[37] In Fallingwater, Wright creates shelter that is founded on the principle of this horizontal freedom and openness rather than the traditional understanding of closure. Yet the sense of shelter so evident even on the outside of Fallingwater comes from the fact that Wright built the house into its site, anchoring it to the earth, our only true shelter. The house provides shelter by opening to its site, rather than by closing itself off. Indeed, in rising from its foundations and opening onto its broad terraces, Fallingwater acts to unfold the sense of shelter latent in the earth itself – that which Wright called *unfolding* architecture as distinguished from *enfolding* architecture. Harrison states: 'if it is to provide this shelter, the earth must be drawn out of its closure by the house ... Wright reminds us that the earth tends to fold into itself, or to withdraw into its own closure, and that the earth cannot become a shelter unless it is unfolded, or disclosed, by human appropriation. It has become clear by now that [for Wright] appropriation does not mean acquisitive possession but the disclosure of freedom in the space of dwelling'.[38]

As we move around the house, our vantage point changes dramatically in height, from above the house to even with it to below it; the horizontal concrete planes and vertical rock walls constantly change position relative to one another, not allowing us to establish any static image of its exterior form. At the first floor, the main horizontal volume sits forward of the main vertical set of walls rising out of the back of the house and cantilevers in both directions parallel to the stream above the falls. The main horizontal volume of the second floor, which serves as the ceiling and roof of the floor below, nevertheless projects perpendicular to the stream bed. These two primary planes cross, one above the other, creating a composite cruciform and capturing the space of the living room at its centre. The third floor is set back, split by the vertical masonry mass, the horizontal planes stretching out to either side and again cantilevering parallel to the stream. As is typical in Wright's houses, we are more aware of the undersides than the tops of the horizontal planes; we sense how they cantilever

29 Final first floor plan.
30 First sketch of south elevation, view from across stream, September 1935. One of the drawings Wright executed while Kaufmann drove the two hours from Milwaukee to Taliesin.
31 Kaufmann guest house at Fallingwater, 1939, elevations.

17

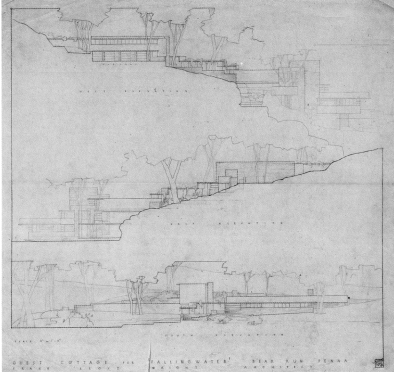

31

32 Final second and third floor plans, west and south elevations.

33 Construction drawings: sections, west and east elevations. As shown, the suspended stairs over the stream were not originally intended to have structural post bearing on stream bed.

34 Construction drawings: sections. As shown, boulder in lower right section C–C was originally intended to be cut off flat. At Kaufmann's suggestion, Wright left it in its existing condition, rounded and emerging from door to form the living room hearth.

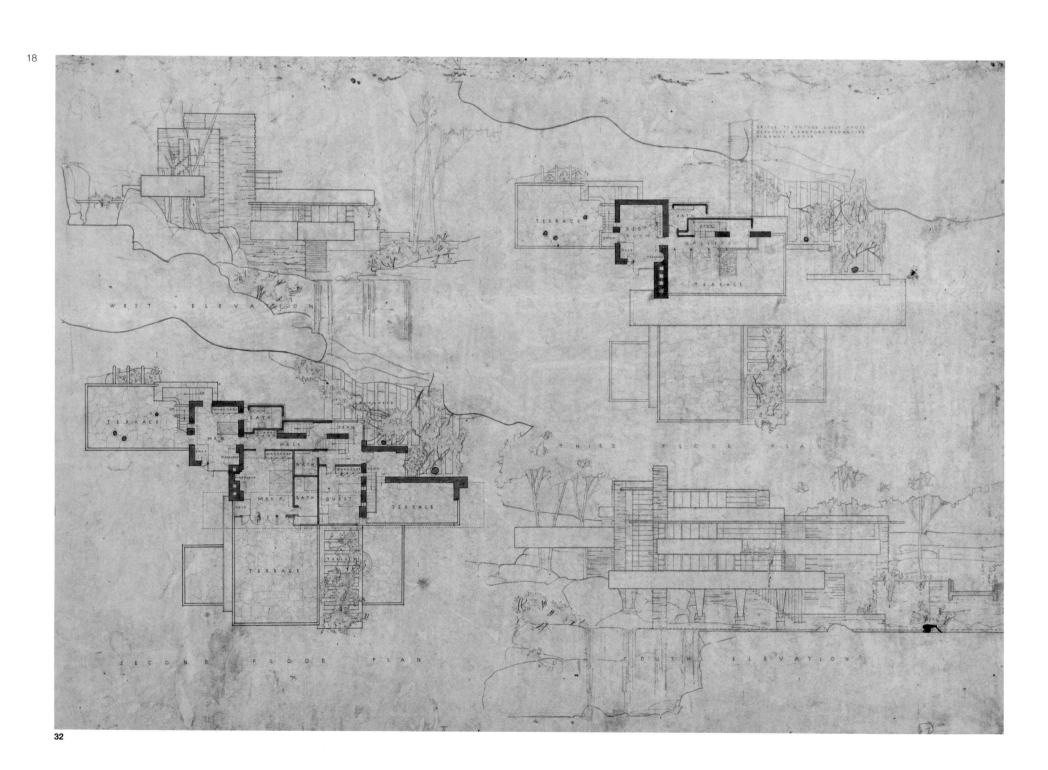

32

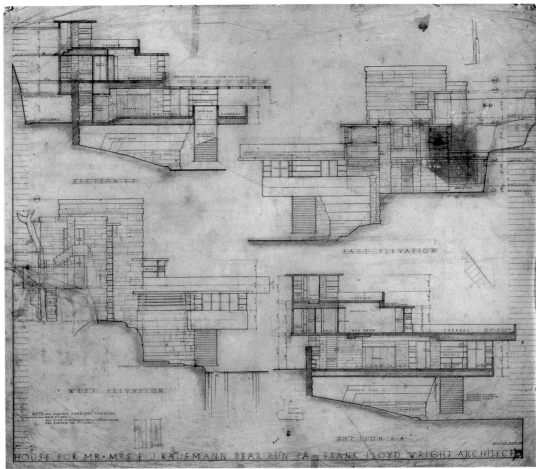

33

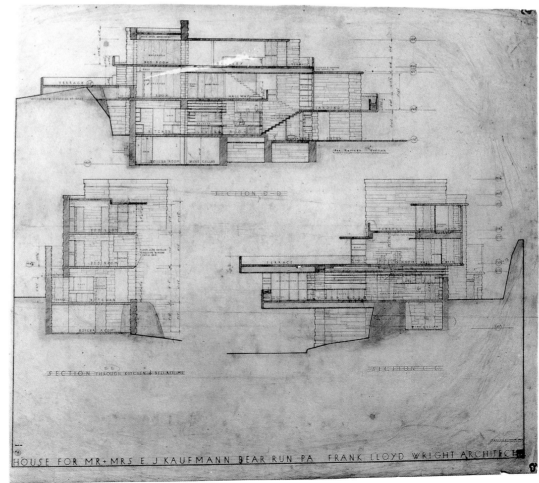

34

35

out to cover space, so that the upper portion of the stream above the falls feels as if it had been drawn into the volume of the house. The house is set against the north side of the stream, cut into a south-facing hillside, so that the sun plays across the three main elevations all day, producing strong shadows, sparkling off the water of the stream, and bringing out the colours of the house's materials. Looking more closely, we notice the glass, set back into the shadows, infilling between the horizontal concrete planes; the red-painted steel mullions only emerge into full view, running in a continuous rhythm up three storeys between the stone walls, when seen from below the waterfall.

In order to enter the house, we must turn away from the vantage point of the famous downstream perspective, walking up along the opposite side of the stream and crossing the bridge that Wright built to the right, or east, side of the house. Wright used an entry road that existed before the house was built as the driveway, which, after crossing this bridge, wraps around and disappears to the left behind the house. The bridge consists of a U-shaped reinforced concrete element, with four square lights set under glass at the corners of the slab, spanning between parallel rock walls on either side of the stream. The view of the house from the bridge is arresting; the darker vertical rock walls are layered one behind the other, stepping up the side of the hill to the right, while the lighter horizontal reinforced concrete slabs and terraces project far out to the left over the stream. The simple span of the bridge on which we stand, supported at both ends, makes us all the more aware of the extent to which the house cantilevers out from its foundations, supported only at one end. The stream is quite shallow here as it moves across the flat face of the bedrock ledge upon which the house sits, and a set of stairs, suspended from the concrete slab above, descend from the living room to a small landing just above the surface of the water. On the right side of the stream, a low wall contains a deep plunge pool carved into the rock, with steps down to it hidden behind the taller rock wall supporting the terrace above. Where Wright has positioned us on the bridge, we can hear the waterfall but not see it as the stream disappears over the edge of the rock ledge at the other end of the house. In order to enter the house and overlook the waterfall from the cantilevered terrace, we cannot approach it directly, as we must move across the bridge. Through its glass wall at our eye-level, we can see directly into and through the living room, floating out over the stream, but as in almost all of Wright's houses, we cannot enter the main room directly, but must move along the edges of the house, around its perimeter, searching for the entrance which is always hidden from the initial view. Utilizing the fact that in architecture the path of the eye can be quite different from the path of the body, Wright lets us catch glimpses of our destination, inviting us to enter the house and rediscover from within what we have first seen or heard from without.

The experience of Fallingwater from within

We cross the bridge and turn left, seeing that the driveway, cut into the natural rock wall of the hill behind before Fallingwater was built, runs between the hillside and the stepped series of rock walls at the back of the house. A trellis of reinforced concrete spans from the rock walls of the house to the rock wall of the hillside, its beams curved occasionally to allow trees existing on the site before the house was built to pass through it undisturbed. To the left an opening between the layered rock walls lets us into a loggia: to the left is a view through suspended concrete stairs to the living room terrace; to the right a small fountain shoots a thin stream of water into a basin set into the earth. Ahead is the front door, made like the windows of glass set in red steel frames, deeply recessed between rock walls, a concrete slab header forming a low ceiling over the entry, the glass above coming forward. As Hoffmann notes, 'Wright's feeling for the site was so keen that the act of crossing the bridge (a span of 28 feet) and approaching the entrance of the house (60 feet past the bridge) would always seem an uphill journey into a private territory, even though the entrance (at three steps below the living room floor) was at an elevation only six inches higher than the bridge roadway'.[39]

Opening the door we move into a small foyer, rock walls directly ahead and to our right; we turn to the opening at the left, towards the living room. Before mounting the three stairs up to the living room floor, we should notice that from the level of this lower foyer, our eye-level is almost exactly at the centre of the space between floor and ceiling. From this brief vantage point, the two horizontal planes are perfectly balanced, the smooth white plaster ceiling above and the rippling dark flagstone floor below, seeming to completely define the space, with only the thin steel mullions of the windows and two square stone piers standing between them – no walls can be seen save those that enclose us at the entry. From this perspective, the living room seems to open out in all directions, so that upon passing through the small cave-like entry we find, much to our surprise, that we can look out to the trees on on all sides. Rising only slightly at the room's centre to house recessed lighting, Hoffmann points out how 'the lower ceiling plane near the brighter walls of glass at the perimeter would give a certain velocity to the outward flow of space, toward broad horizontal vistas'.[40] Moving up the three steps, we are struck by the difference our higher viewpoint makes in our perception of the living room; the ceiling (only seven feet one inch in height) is now very close to our heads and the flagstone floor now dominates our view. With the light coming towards us from the windows all around, the reflections off the flagstone floor make it appear strikingly similar to the water of the stream below.

Upon entering the living room, we are surrounded by low walls with built-in bookcases, desks and long seats, the only exception being the glass doors diagonally across the room. Drawn towards the sound of the waterfall, we walk across the living room and open these glass doors, moving out onto the terrace cantilevered out over the waterfall. Looking out into the trees, the sound of the waterfall now surrounds us and we seem now to be a part of it, having been projected out into space directly above. At this moment we recognize Wright's intention in placing the house where he did; rather than present the waterfall as an object to be looked at, he allows us to feel as if we are part of it, hearing it and sensing it, but rarely seeing it from within the house. The American philosopher

35 Living room. Diagonal view towards fireplace and dining table, as seen from top of 'hatch' or suspended stairs.

36 Construction drawings: glass hatch over suspended stairs at living room; plan, elevation and section.

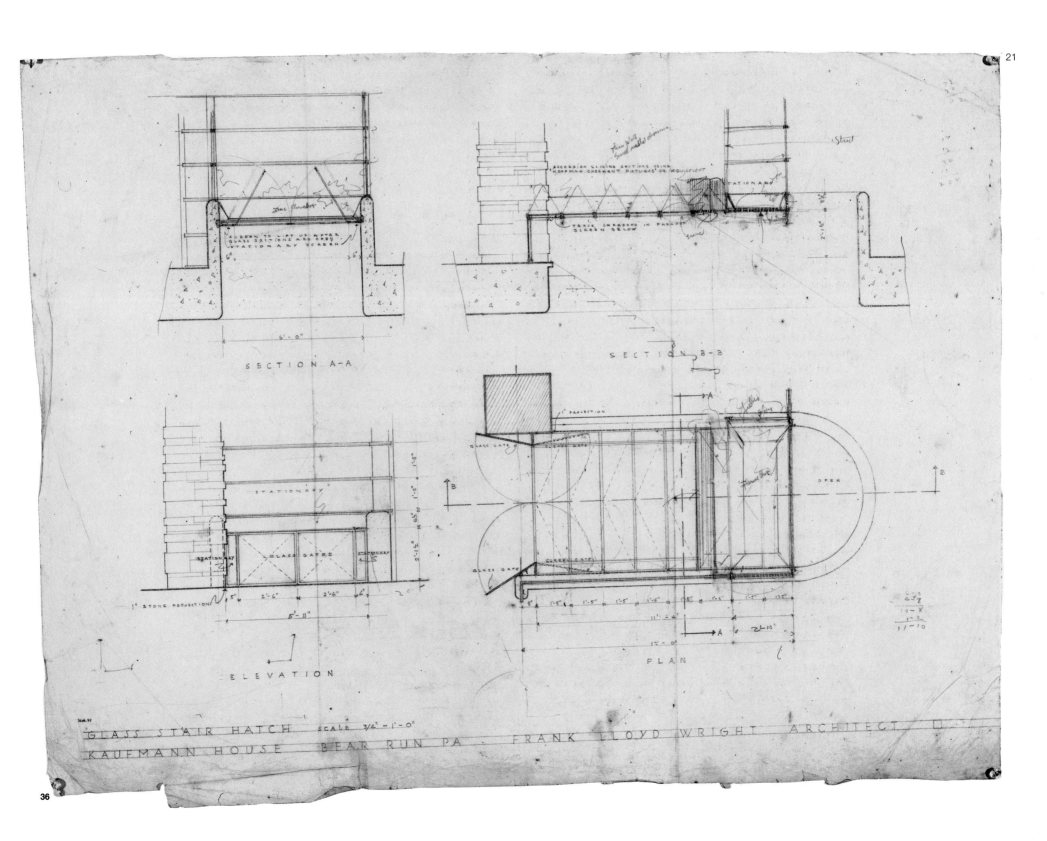

John Dewey has noted that 'the eye is the sense of distance', while 'sound itself is near, intimate;'[41] Wright himself actively engages this difference in our experience of Fallingwater. In this way, the waterfall never becomes merely an image for the house's inhabitants, as it does in the famous perspectival view from below, but remains something that underlies our entire experience, permeating all of our senses, including most strongly our hearing and our haptic sense – the sense of bodily position and movement in space.

This feeling of being suspended over the waterfall is reinforced and confirmed as we are drawn back into the room towards the bright light coming from the trellis and skylights opened in the concrete roof directly ahead; a low glass-enclosed 'hatch' opens to the concrete stair that we saw earlier descending to the stream below. The dark grey colour of the bedrock ledge under the shallow water, and the way light is reflected from the rippling surface of the stream, are matched exactly by the grey flagstone floor upon which we stand. Seen through the hatch, the suspended stairs oppose the flow of the water in the stream, and the movement down to the water is balanced by the skylight and trellis openings to the sky above. Descending to the stream below, we enter the large exterior space covered by the main concrete floor slab of the house, only ten feet above the surface of the stream. Behind us to our left, seen through the open risers of the stair, are the three piers angled out to support the house above, the dark space underneath the house open all the way back to the boulders of the hillside. Ahead is the bridge, to the left the rock walls, plunge pool and sculpture, to the right the natural stream bank; we are hovering only inches above the water, facing away from the waterfall, roaring behind us.

Ascending the stairs and emerging again into the living room, we turn to the right; diagonally across the room is the fireplace: large, heavy, its fire flickering from the darkness of the rock walls anchoring the back of the house. This fireplace is not set into the wall – it *is* the wall, a half-cylinder cavity running from floor to plaster soffit, the hearth the boulder of the site itself, emerging from the floor; Hoffmann notes: 'Indoors the [flagstones of the floor] were sealed and waxed, but the boulder was not. It came through the floor like the dry top of a boulder peering above the stream waters'.[42] A red spherical kettle is set into a hemispherical niche in the stone to one side, suspended on a steel pivot that allows it to be swung over the fire. The buffet is built in along the back wall under a high window to the right of the fireplace, and the built-in dining table, centred exactly on the main volume of the living room that projects out across the stream, similarly projects from the back wall into the room itself. We are now aware that within the rectangular volume of this room, centred by the two stone piers that make a square with the entry wall and fireplace, there is a counter-pointing pair of strong diagonal axes: that between the stair down to the stream and the fireplace, both vertically-oriented (water-sky and rock-sky) and opening on the edge of the primary volume of the living room; and that between the entry and the terrace over the waterfall, both horizontally-oriented and contained in volumes projected off the corners of the primary volume of the living room (together creating a pinwheel with the living room). These two axes between four pivotal 'places' within the house give the cruciform geometric volumes of the whole a diagonal pattern of use or inhabitation, reinforced by the fact that, as is typical in Wright's houses, the doors into the room open at its corners.

In the corner between the fireplace and dining table is the door to the kitchen, which is enclosed on almost all sides by the stone walls anchoring the house to its site. The light in the kitchen comes from the stacked horizontal windows that turn a corner, leaving space for a narrow casement. The view out from this cave-like kitchen to the terrace floating over the waterfall, set at the same floor level, gives the most succinct experience of the oppositions Wright built into and balanced in this house. This is again encountered in the stairs which climb up between stone walls to the second floor, beginning across from the kitchen door, behind the entry foyer. What we might normally expect to find – the heavier falling towards the ground and the lighter rising towards the sky – is reversed when we notice that the solid, heavy, stone stairs go *up*, while the open, light, concrete stairs at the hatch go *down*. That this is not coincidental becomes evident when we see that the points where the two stairs start their respective ascent and descent from the flagstone floor are aligned along the same edge of the living room, suggesting that Wright intended us to perceive the stairs as the two sides of a single experience of gravitational reversal made possible by the cantilevered, hillside section of the house, grounded by the flagstone floor of the living room. Our penetration down through the stone floor to find light stairs floating over water which reflects the sky overhead, combined with our penetration up through layers of solid stone to finally emerge, unexpectedly, at the tree-tops rather than at their roots, make this one of the most astonishing and richly suggestive movement sequences in all of Wright's work.

The second floor hall leads to the master bedroom, the fireplace of which exhibits the most dynamic stonework in the entire house. The large rectangular stones of the mantel and adjacent shelves cantilever asymmetrically towards the hearth in a manner similar to the way the house as a whole projects out over the stream. Through glass doors opens a terrace far larger than the bedroom itself; the scale of this terrace demands that it be understood as the second 'great room' of the house – an outdoor room above the living room, with unencumbered views out in three directions. From this vantage point, we can see that the flagstone floors of the house and terraces, so similar to the water's surface, repeat at higher and higher levels the layered planes begun by the two horizontal surfaces of the stream, below and above the falls – just as the rock walls extend the rock layers of the stream bed outcroppings. The large volume of the terrace is complemented by the subtlety of Wright's use of wood graining along the opposite wall; the door into the master bedroom has the wood grain running vertically from floor to ceiling, while the built-in cupboards and cabinets, cantilevered off the wall with four inches left open at top and bottom, have the wood grain running horizontally. This reminds us of the similar ordering of the window mullions in the house; the operable doors and windows have vertical proportions while the fixed windows have horizontal proportions, often with butt-glazing at the corners to eliminate the vertical member altogether.

37 Preliminary west elevation of living room, looking towards fireplace and kitchen door.

38 Preliminary construction drawing: suspended stairs below glass hatch at living room; plan, elevation and structural details. Note addition of structural post bearing on stream bed.

39 Preliminary design drawing for living room fireplace. Plan and elevation with swinging kettle shown in both 'in' and 'out' positions.

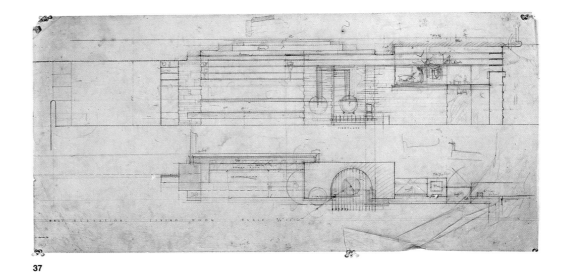

37

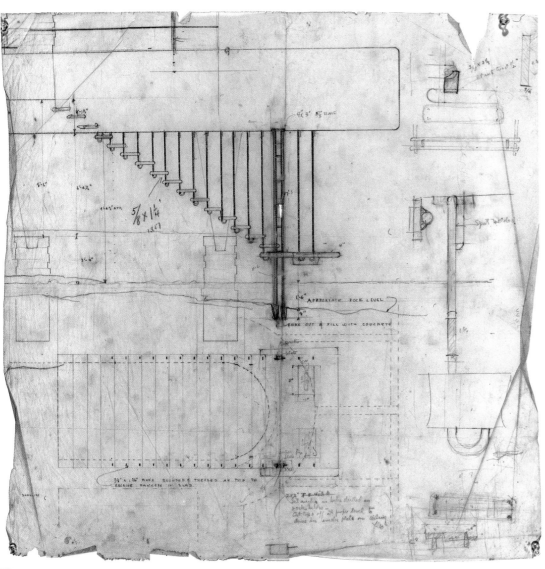

38

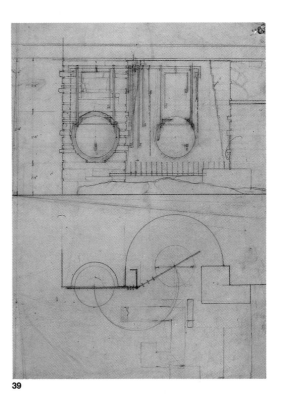

39

The bedroom used by Mr Kaufmann is over the kitchen, with the same sense of cave-like, rock-walled refuge. Up a few stairs at the back a long terrace cantilevers to the west of the house, anchoring to a freestanding boulder with a series of concrete ribs. The stair to the third floor has wooden bookshelves set into the horizontal joints of the stonework, similar to shelves appearing above the fireplace and dining table in the living room. On the third floor is a long gallery facing a smaller terrace, and the bedroom used by Edgar Kaufmann, Jr, sits above that used by his father, with which its shares the west terrace. In both of these small bedrooms and in the kitchen, the stonework of the fireplace wall seems to pass right through the glass from inside to outside, due to Wright's careful provision of a vertical slot between the stones that allows the glass to be set directly into the stone, without any kind of frame; there is no more telling detail in Fallingwater, and Wright's intention 'to bring the outside world into the house and let the inside of the house go outside'[43] is here given its perfect interpretation. In these rooms he also achieves the perfect open corner, for the corner is made by two small casement windows which, when opened, cause the corner to disappear altogether. In these small rooms, the irregular horizontal layers of the stone walls are integrated with the regular horizontal rhythm of the steel window mullions and the shifting wooden planes of the built-in bookshelves and tabletops to produce a true sense of shelter, combining the attributes of refuge and outlook.[44]

Fallingwater appears to us to have grown out of the ground and into the light, making present the latent power of the boulder on which it sits above the waterfall – the same boulder which emerges from the rippling 'water' of the flagstone living room floor to provide a place of stability in front of the fireplace. The natural setting is so integrated into this house that in occupying it we are constantly reminded of where we are by the sound of the waterfall, the flow of space and movement inside and outside across the floors and terraces, the fire burning in the bedrock masonry of the house giving a sense of refuge, while the views and sunlight are framed by the steel windows, which act as spatial 'nets' or 'webs' similar to the weaving of stained glass in Wright's earlier houses. The whole is carefully calibrated to the scale and eye-level of the inhabitant; the degree to which Wright formed his designs to respond to human comfort and the rituals of daily life is rarely acknowledged, despite his statement that 'human use and comfort should not be taxed to pay dividends on any designer's idiosyncrasy. Human use and comfort should have intimate possession of every interior – should be felt in every exterior'.[45] Particularly in the living room, the primary room of the house containing entry, library, living and dining, Fallingwater appears to us as a place that calls for inhabitation; it seems empty and meaningless without the human figure occupying its spaces, acting out the rituals of daily life. In what sounds remarkably like a description of Fallingwater, Dewey described an ideal relation between architecture, dwelling and landscape by saying: 'Through going out into the environment, position unfolds into volume; through the pressure of environment, mass is retracted into energy of position, and space remains, when matter is contracted, as an opportunity for further action'.[46]

The rediscovery of fundamental dwelling

Lillian Kaufmann once sent Wright a birthday card in which she wrote: 'Living in a house built by you has been my one education'.[47] In Fallingwater Wright captured the perfect essence of our desire to live with nature, to dwell in a forested place and be at home in the natural world. Edgar Kaufmann, Jr, on the day he donated Fallingwater to the public after living in it for 25 years, said: 'Its beauty remains fresh like that of the nature into which it fits. It has served well as a house, yet has always been more that that: a work of art, beyond any ordinary measures of excellence ... House and site together form the very image of man's desire to be at one with nature, equal and wedded to nature ... Such a place cannot be possessed'.[48] To visit Fallingwater, as to live in it, is an education in the potential of architectural design. We cannot help feeling that the house is intended as the setting for communing with nature: the stairs down to the stream; the boulder-hearth emerging from the flagstone floor; and the all-permeating sound of the waterfall confirm this initial impression. We are not the same after occupying it as we were when we entered; our perceptions have been both broadened and deepened, our experience has been profoundly moving; yet we are aware, Hoffmann notes, that Fallingwater 'reveals itself slowly, and never once and for all'.[49]

Fallingwater opened a new chapter in American architecture, and is perhaps rightly considered Wright's greatest work, for he was first and foremost an architect of houses. In its careful yet startling integration of ancient stone walls anchored to the bedrock and modern reinforced concrete terraces hovering in space, Connors states that Fallingwater may be understood as 'one of the great critiques of the modern movement in architecture, and simultaneously one of its masterpieces'.[50] Yet we cannot help feeling that there is more to this design than even that; this is an architecture that seizes our imagination, letting us see space and inhabitation in ways that seem new, but which we simultaneously feel to be ancient, somehow fundamental to our human nature. Gaston Bachelard said that 'discoveries made about the structure of space and time always react on the structure of the mind',[51] yet Fallingwater, and indeed all of Wright's work, would perhaps better be thought of as a rediscovery of the possibilities of dwelling in space and time. In this Wright was perhaps one of the only architects of our time to engage fundamental ancient principles in the creation of interior space, seeking the space within which was defined without boundaries; defined instead by the rituals of daily experience. Fallingwater is such a place, hovering among the leaves of the trees yet anchored to the bedrock of the earth, its spaces in flowing motion yet the whole a stable mass read against the movement of the stream; our experience of it that of a cave-like refuge yet also that of a free-floating outlook. As Wright said in 1936: 'An idea (probably rooted deep in instinct) that *shelter* should be the essential look of any dwelling. I came to see a building primarily not as a cave but as a broad shelter in the open, related to vista; vista without and vista within. You may see in these various feelings all taking the same direction that I was born an American, child of the ground and of space'.[52]

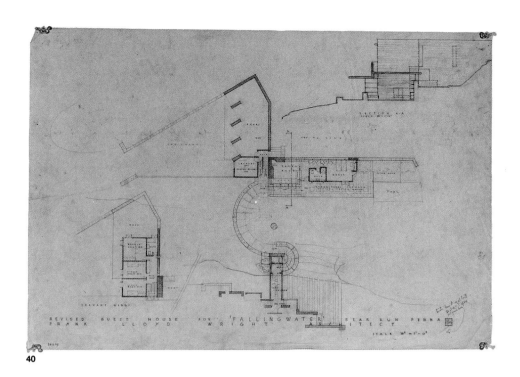

40 Fallingwater guest house
and garage. Final plans and
section.

41 Bridge over drive and
covered walkway from main
house to guest house. Plan,
elevation and sketch perspective
as seen from above.

40

25

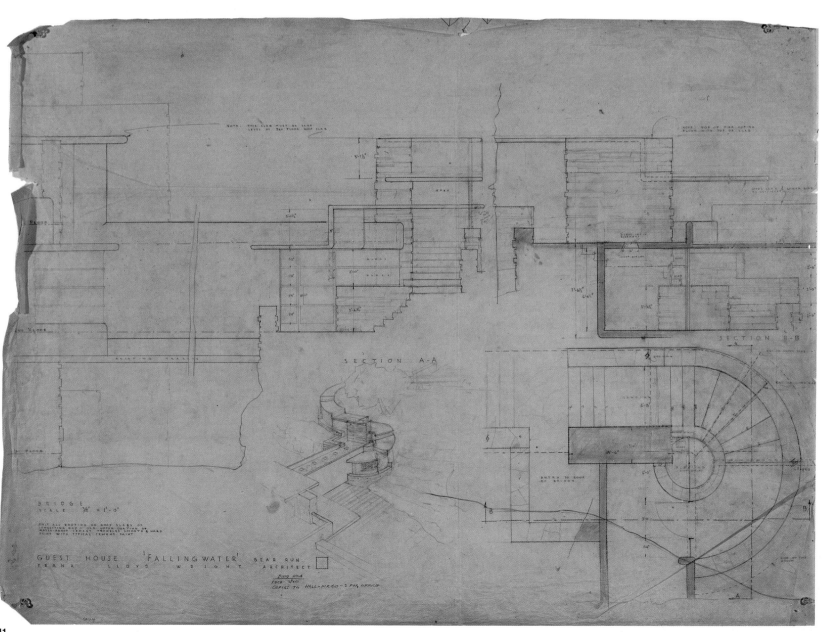

41

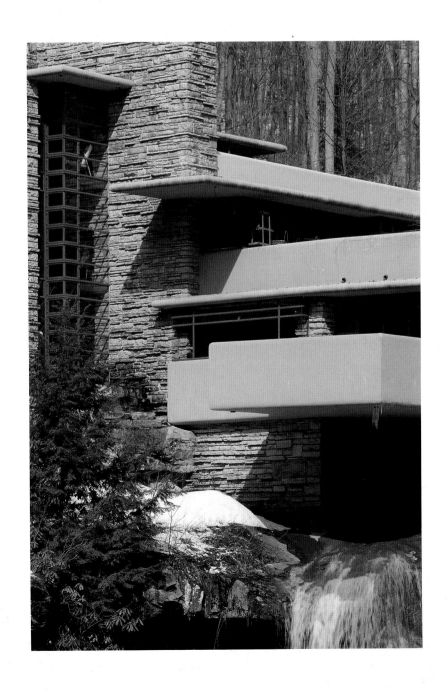

Left and centre Fallingwater
from without. Horizontal planes
projecting from a stone core,
cantilevered out over the waterfall, allowing the occupants to
inhabit a series of layered spaces
starting with the surface of the
stream below, continuing with
the flagstone-covered terraces
floating one above the other,
and terminating in the foliage
of the trees.

Right The house seen through
the trees from the hillside on the
opposite bank of the stream.
Similar to the view first seen in
approaching the house, we are
looking directly into the elevation, which from this vantage
point appears to be composed
of a series of floating horizontal
planes with no apparent means
of support. While the forms of
the house seem suggestive of
motion, the house as a whole is
paradoxically read as stable
against the constant actual
motion of the stream that
flows beneath it.

Fallingwater takes on differing readings with the changing seasons; spring, summer, autumn and winter each bring out specific aspects of the design, from the emphasis on the horizontal stacked stone and terraces when they are covered with snow, to the golden colour of the concrete and red of the steel window mullions which echo the leaves in autumn.

Left Views of the covered walkway leading from the main house to the guest house, an astonishingly agile, asymmetrical, folded, reinforced concrete structure that leads in a spiral up the hill to the guest house above.
Right The terrace on the guest house looks out to the south over the main house, and is covered by a low roof, with trellis-like openings, which terminates the folded roof over the walkway.

32

From the entry bridge, the solid vertical stone wall anchors the house to the right as the concrete planes project out over the stream to the left. While its sound is powerfully present, the waterfall cannot be seen from this vantage point, and we must enter the house to experience both the stream, on the stairs suspended just above its surface, and the waterfall itself, which can only be seen looking over the terrace on the other side of the living room from where we stand – thus we are invited to enter the house.

The composition of powerful anchorage and support, palpably present in the beams buried in the rock outcropping behind the upper bedroom terrace, and spaces suspended without any visible means of support, as in the terrace floating out over the waterfall (here seen from above), exemplifies the extraordinary capacity of this house to condense and make present the experiential possibilities of architectural construction.

Left and centre Views towards the entry, with neighbouring music alcove, and a detail of the concrete header shelf over the glass front door.
Right View from the kitchen door towards the entry, at right, and stone stairs up to second floor, at left, with dining table in the foreground.

Left The hearth of the living room fireplace is the top of the bedrock boulder which rises right through the flagstone floor like a dry rock breaking through the surface of the stream. The boulder originally remained unwaxed, so that it literally appeared dry next to the waxed and reflective flagstones. The spherical kettle swings out of its hemispherical niche in the stone fireplace wall and hangs over the fire, allowing drinks to be heated.

Centre Diagonally across the living room from the fireplace is the glass 'hatch' covering the stairs suspended over the surface of the stream. From this vantage point we become aware that the surface of the stream and the waxed flagstones of the floor upon which we stand are exactly the same colour and texture.

Right The oppositions between anchorage and projection are powerfully summarized in the view from the kitchen, where we stand within a cave-like room made of rock and look towards the terrace suspended out into space over the waterfall.

The living room is defined by the shimmering, water-like flagstone floors and the smooth, precise, light ceiling floating overhead – each of these surfaces, while constructed of heavy materials, seems transformed by the space and light flowing and floating under and over us. Sunlight and exterior views enter all around as the walls are largely dissolved into glass curtains, allowing us to be suspended over stream or water-fall, while simultaneously being housed within this refuge anchored into the earth.

Left The second floor bedroom of Edgar Kaufmann has a built-in wood desk with a quarter circle cut out to allow the casement window to open, and bookshelves are let into the joints in the stone.

Centre and far right The master bedroom, used by Lillian Kaufmann, has a built-in closet with the wood grains ordered to complement the vertical and horizontal patterns of the window mullions of the house, and a fireplace that interlocks with the built-in desk, exhibiting the most dynamic stonework in the entire house. The stone stairs leading to the third floor are flanked by wooden bookshelves that are spaced on the pattern of the stair treads.

Right The guest house contains a single expansive room, the bedroom screened by the bathroom block, the entry demarcated from the living room by a simple wall of open wood slats, and the whole lined to the north by a narrow band of high clerestory windows, providing cooling cross-ventilation.

44

Left In Edgar Kaufmann's bedroom (and in the study above), the glass of the windows is set directly into the stone wall, without framing at the edge. This detail, perhaps more than any other, summarizes Wright's intentions for this house through the way in which it brings the outside in and the inside out, and in the manner in which it juxtaposes opposite formal, structural, material and experiential aspects of architecture – in this case the delicate, light, ephemeral glass pushing into the rough, heavy, rustic stone wall.

Below The third floor gallery – later made his bedroom by Edgar Kaufmann, Jr – compresses this experience of opposites, bringing into close proximity the horizontal extension and release from gravity, found on the terraces cantilevered out into the treetops, and the vertical anchorage and celebration of gravity, found in the stacked bedrock slabs that comprise the room's rear walls. In all these experiences, this house, a paradoxical space of resolved oppositions, finally reveals itself as a primal homage to the site and a place for ritual communion with nature.

Site plan
1 main home
2 guest house and garage
3 entry drive

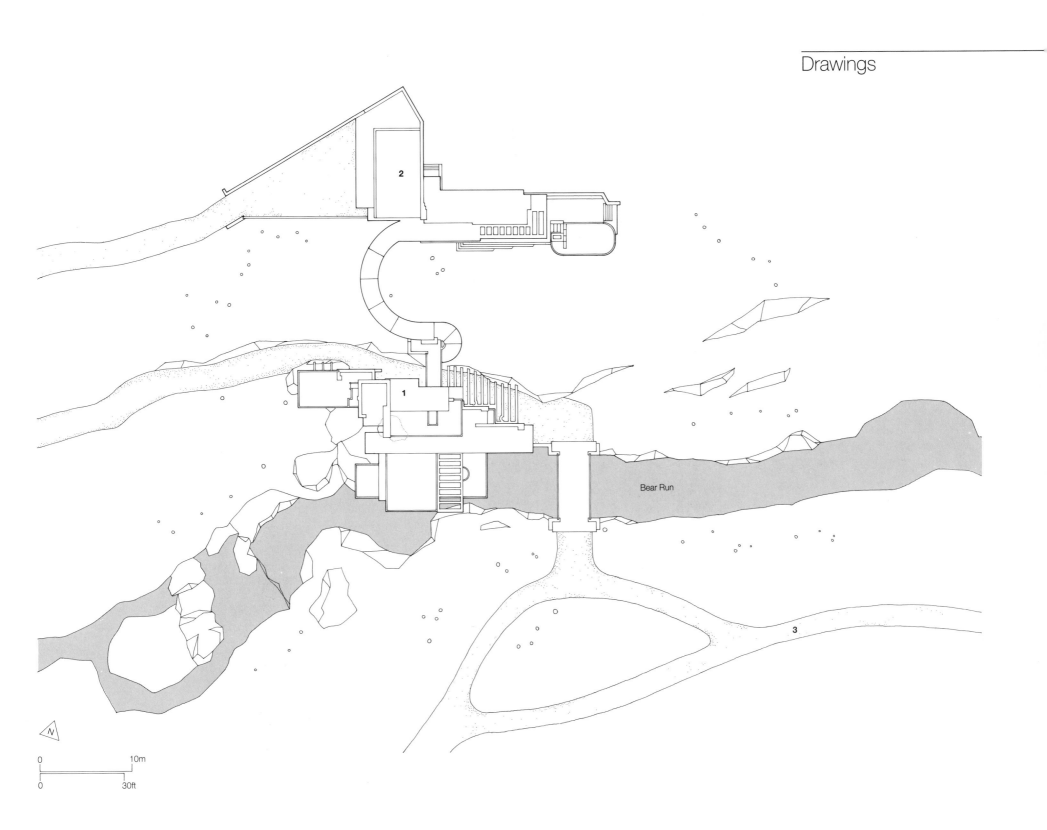

2

1

Bear Run

3

N

0   10m

0   30ft

Floor plans

48

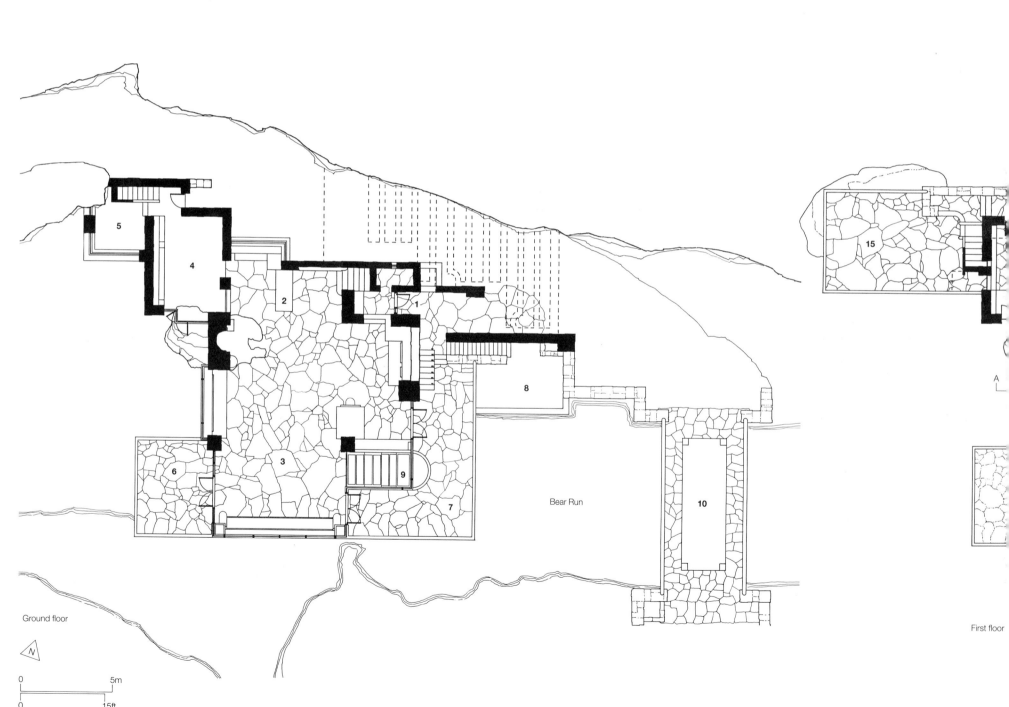

Bear Run

Ground floor

First floor

0 ——— 5m

0 ——— 15ft

N

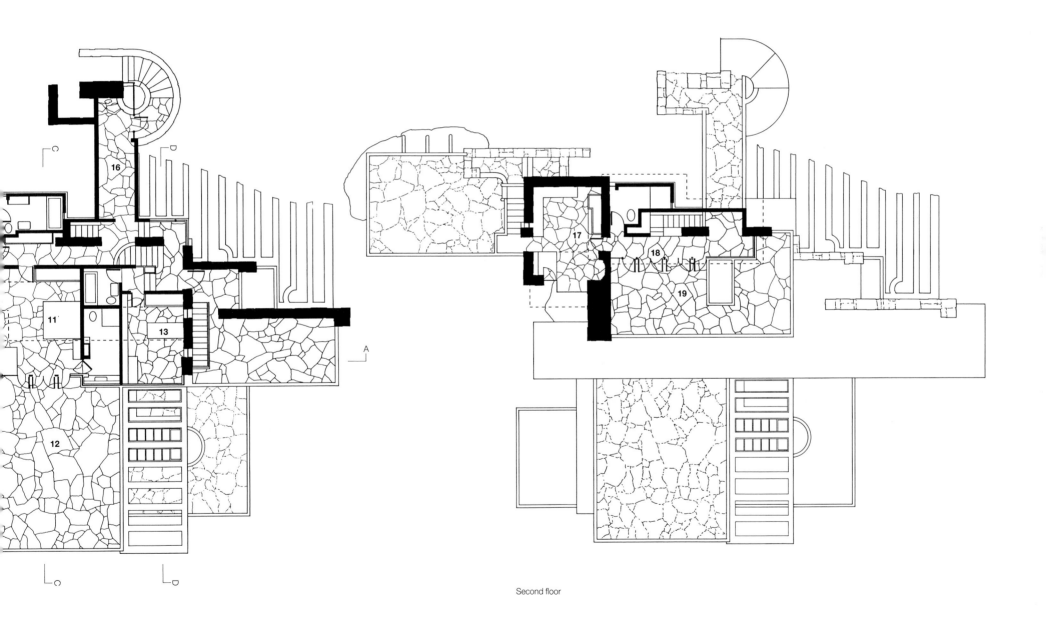

Second floor

50

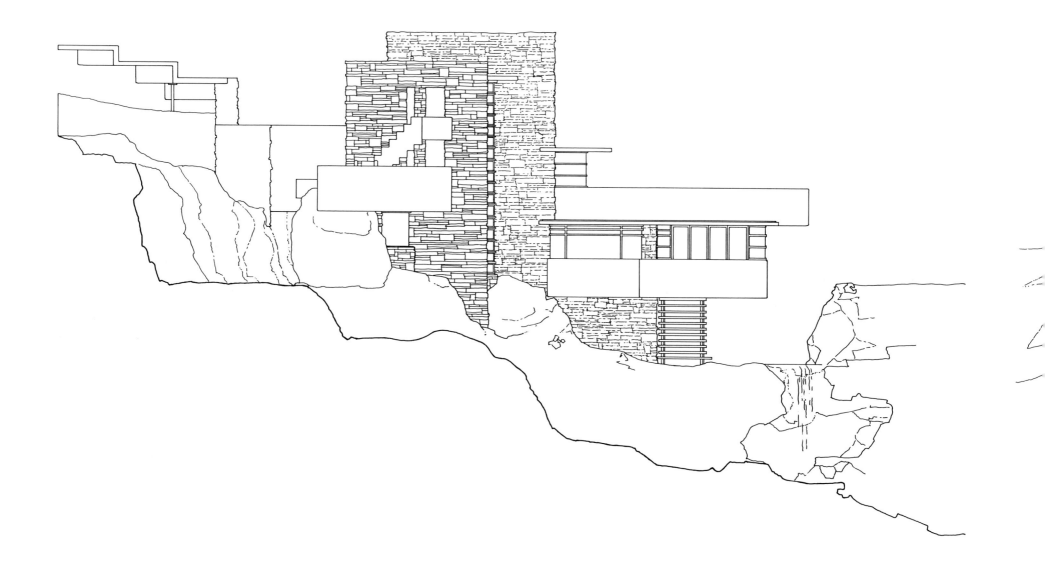

52

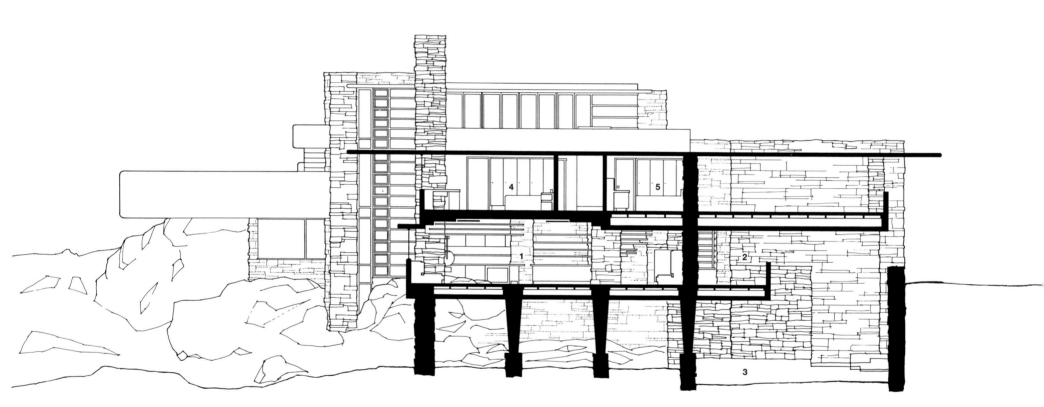

Section AA looking north

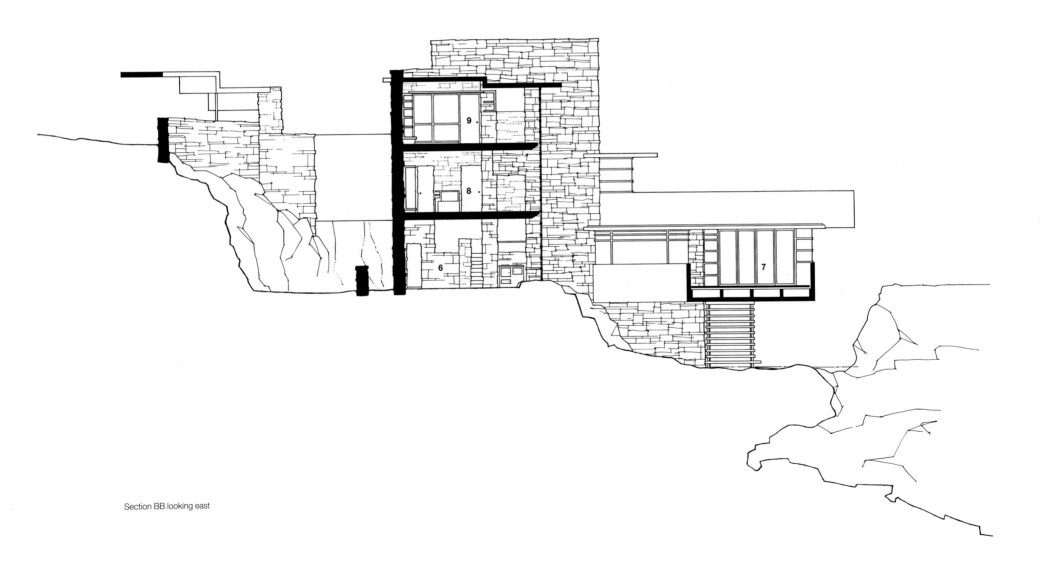

Section BB looking east

Sections

1 dining room
2 living room
3 master bedroom
4 master bedroom terrace
5 gallery
6 gallery terrace
7 east living room terrace
8 guest bedroom
9 gallery terrace

54

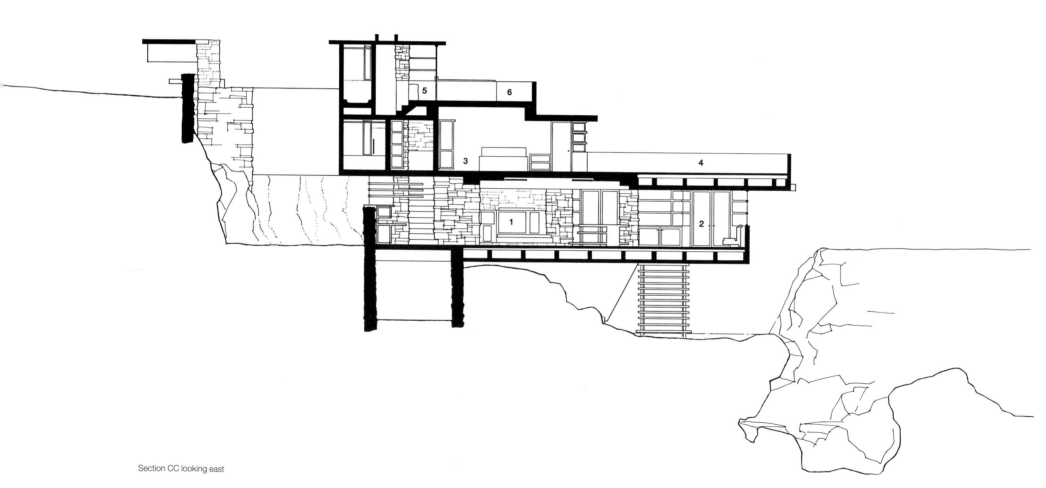

Section CC looking east

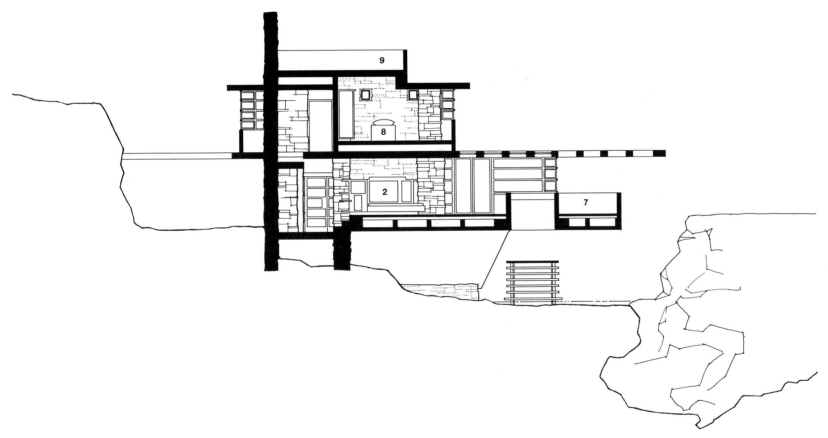

Section DD looking east

Living room

1 bookshelves
2 table
3 cupboard
4 seat
5 stairs
6 lamp standard
7 radiator
8 hatch

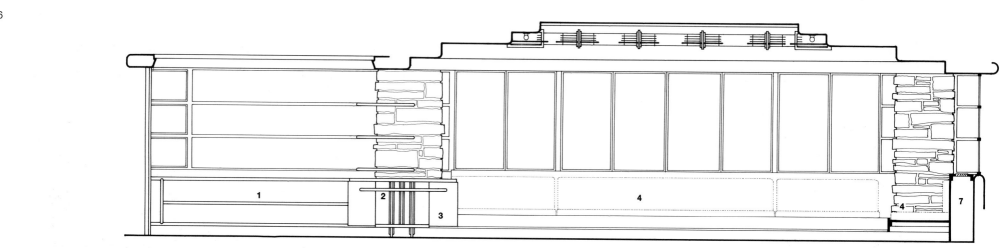

South elevation

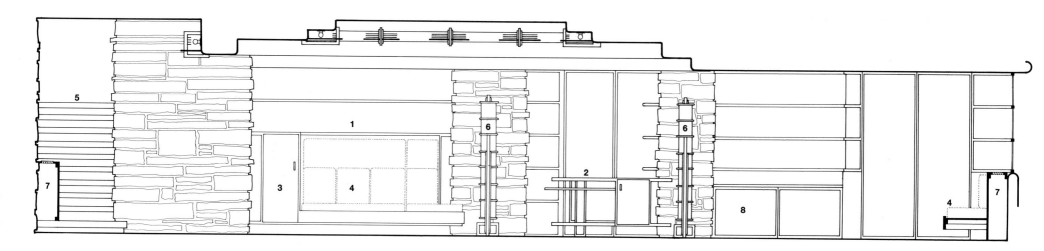

East elevation

Living room hearth with wine kettle

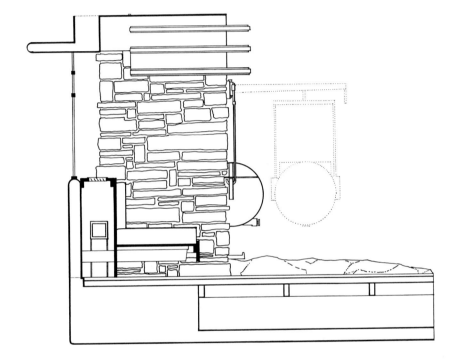

Section

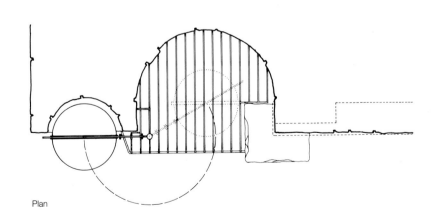

Elevation

Plan

0 ⊢———⊣ 1m

0 ⊢———⊣ 3ft

Author's acknowledgements

58   I would like to thank the following people, whose efforts were essential to the completion of this book: The new drawings prepared for this publication were made by Robert Blatter and James Buzbee, who, along with fourteen other undergraduate and graduate students in the University of Florida's Department of Architecture, participated in a seminar I taught on Wright's drawings during the summer of 1993. Cathy Duncan, another participant in that seminar, researched and secured reproduction rights for photographic and drawing material used in this publication. Edward Teague, Librarian for the University of Florida Fine Arts and Architecture Library, provided information used in assembling the bibliography. Of the sources of illustrations, I would in particular like to thank Oscar Munoz, of the Frank Lloyd Wright Archives, who provided reproductions of Wright's drawings, and Janet Parks and Angela Giral of the Avery Architectural Library at Columbia University, who made available important photographic material. The published research of Donald Hoffmann and recollections of Edgar Kaufmann, Jr, are essential reading for anyone wishing to understand in depth the history of Fallingwater, and I have drawn upon them regularly in this text. I must thank my fellow faculty members and my students, who have endured a sometimes distracted department chair and teacher during the period I was writing this and other texts on Wright, and I owe many thanks to Dean Wayne Drummond, who has supported my perhaps atypical activity. Finally, thanks to James Steele, on whose recommendation I became involved in this project.

Illustration sources

(Numbers quoted refer to figure numbers, unless otherwise stated.) Avery Architectural and Fine Arts Library and Archives, Columbia University, New York: 11, 25, 26, 27, 28; Carnegie Institute Museum of Art, Chicago Chicago Historical Society (photograph Hedrich Blessing): 7; Fallingwater/Western Pennsylvania Conservancy: 9, 10, and colour photographs p 31 (photographs by Robert P Ruschak and Thomas A Heinz); Donald Hoffmann: 5; Frank Lloyd Wright Archives, copyright Frank Lloyd Wright Foundation, 1993: 1, 2, 3, 4, 12, 13, 14, 15, 16, 17, 18, 19, 20, 21, 22, 23, 24, 29, 30, 31, 32, 33, 34, 36, 37, 38, 39, 40, 41.

Notes

1 George Steiner, *Tolstoy or Dostoevsky*, New York: Vintage/Random House, 1959, p 3.

2 Joseph Connors, *The Robie House of Frank Lloyd Wright*, Chicago: University of Chicago Press, 1984, p 63.

3 Brendan Gill, *Many Masks: A Life of Frank Lloyd Wright*, New York: Putnam's, 1987, p 326.

4 Edgar Kaufmann, Jr, *Fallingwater: A Frank Lloyd Wright Country House*, New York: Abbeville Press, 1986, p 36. The younger Kaufmann, never having intended to be an architect, went on to become an important art historian, and one of Wright's chief interpreters. This beautifully-illustrated book gives his own recollections of the history of the house with which he was so closely associated.

5 Donald Hoffmann, *Frank Lloyd Wright's Fallingwater, The House and Its History*, New York: Dover, 1978, pp 8–10. Most of the factual information on the site, design and construction of Fallingwater used herein is drawn from this book, which is the definitive historical study of this house. Hoffmann's exhaustive investigation of the history of Fallingwater is essential reading for those desiring the full story of this extraordinary building.

6 Frank Lloyd Wright, *In the Cause of Architecture* (1928). F Gutheim, ed, reprint of *Architectural Record* essays, New York: McGraw-Hill, 1975, p 153.

7 For the various versions, see Hoffmann, op cit, pp 15–17. For Mosher and Tafel's version, as well as Tafel's memories of the construction, see Edgar Tafel, *Apprentice to Genius: Years with Frank Lloyd Wright* (1979), reprint, New York: Dover, 1985, pp 1–9.

8 Hoffmann, op cit, p 17.

9 Blaine Drake, an apprentice, recalls this in a letter quoted in Hoffmann, op cit, p 15.

10 Bob Mosher, in a 1974 letter quoted in Hoffmann, op cit, p 17.

11 Wright, in an interview with Hugh Downs, 1953, Frank Lloyd Wright, *The Future of Architecture*, New York: Horizon, 1953, p 16. This distinction between the experience of nearness and distance is fully developed by the philosopher Martin Heidegger; see his *Basic Writings*, New York: Harper and Row, 1977.

12 Connors, op cit, p 61.

13 In the late 1980s the Taliesin Fellowship and FLW Foundation, in an attempt to raise funds to pay back taxes and to support the (unaccredited) FLW School at Taliesin, sold, through the Max Protetch Gallery in New York, numerous important early sketches by Wright. Among these were these four earliest design perspectives; sketchy and faint, in coloured pencils executed by Wright himself, we could see the design emerging in these drawings, not yet perfected, but in process – a rare moment indeed. Unfortunately, these four drawings are no longer available for study, having been purchased for more than $40,000 by private collectors. The FLW Foundation claimed these were 'unimportant', but what they apparently meant was they were design sketches, as they held onto the finished renderings which were generally not from Wright's hand, letting the far more important design sketches be sold. This was a serious failure on the part of the Taliesin Fellowship and FLW Foundation, which is charged with preserving, not selling off, Wright's drawings.

14 Wright, *Frank Lloyd Wright: On Architecture*, ed F Gutheim, New York: Grosset and Dunlap, 1941, p 232.

15 Wright, *In the Cause of Architecture* (1908), p 61. This is quoted in Connors' insightful study of the Robie House, op cit, where he finds three precedents within Wright's own work for the Robie House – for which again we have no surviving sketch studies.

16 Hoffmann, op cit, p 73.

17 Connors, op cit, p 61.

18 Documented and analyzed in Paul Laseau and James Tice, *Frank Lloyd Wright: Between Principle and Form*, New York: Van Nostrand Reinhold, 1992, p 34. Werner Seligmann has written an essay giving a full analysis of Fallingwater and its relation to the earlier Prairie Houses; we can only hope that this important work will one day be published.

19 One such incident, that of Wright's having holes cut in the balcony of the Robie House, is detailed by Joseph Connors, op cit, p 26.

20 This almost theatrical ability of Wright to choreograph the construction process towards his own ends is perhaps best seen in the famous sequence of structural tests he agreed to allow to be performed by the sceptical state engineers and building inspectors on the innovative 'mushroom' columns of the Johnson Wax Administration Building; see Jonathan Lipman, *Frank Lloyd Wright and the Johnson Wax Buildings*, New York: Rizzoli, 1986, pp 59–62.

21 Hoffmann, op cit, p 21.

22 Hoffmann, op cit, p 24.

23 Hoffmann, op cit, p 33.

24 Hoffmann, op cit, p 49.

25 The house and 1,543 acres of land was donated by Edgar Kaufmann, Jr, to the Western Pennsylvania Conservancy on October 29, 1963. For tours of Fallingwater, reservations and information are available from the Conservancy at PO Box R, Mill Run, Pennsylvania 15464; tel 412-329-8501.

26 Hoffmann, op cit, p 6.

27 Beautifully documented in photographs by Henry Hamilton Bennett and written about in Thomas Beeby, 'Wright and Landscape: A Mythical Interpretation', *The Nature of Frank Lloyd Wright*, ed Bolon, Nelson, Seidel, Chicago: University of Chicago Press, 1988, pp 154–72.

28 Robert P Harrison, *Forests, The Shadow of Civilization*, Chicago: Chicago University Press, 1992, p 232. Harrison's insightful discussion of Fallingwater's relation to the forest and to the landscape is far more inspiring and accurate, I believe, than the continuing efforts to see Fallingwater as yet another country house or villa in the classical tradition.

29 Harrison, op cit, p 232.

30 Frank Lloyd Wright, *The Natural House*, New York: Horizon, 1954, p 44.

31 Wright, *The Future of Architecture*, pp 321–2.

32 Wright, *In the Cause of Architecture* (1928), p 177.

33 Heidegger, 'Building Dwelling Thinking' (1951), in *Basic Writings*, op cit, p 330.

34 A phrase used by the contemporary Swiss-Italian architect Mario Botta.

35 Wright, *The Natural House*, p 58.

36 Frank Lloyd Wright, *An Autobiography*, New York: Horizon, 1977, p 164.

37 Harrison, op cit, p 233.

38 Harrison, op cit, pp 234–5. In this analysis, Harrison is indebted to Heidegger's various essays that address dwelling and architecture.

39 Hoffmann, op cit, p 27.

40 Hoffmann, op cit, p 39.

41 John Dewey, *Art as Experience* (1932), New York: Putnam's, 1980, p 237.

42 Hoffmann, op cit, p 56.

43 Wright, *An Autobiography*, p 166.

44 Categories necessary for a sense of dwelling to unfold, according to the theory of landscape proposed by Jay Appleton in his *The Experience of Landscape* and extensively utilized by Grant Hildebrandt in his *The Wright Space: Pattern and Meaning in Frank Lloyd Wright's Houses*, Seattle: University of Washington Press, 1991.

45 Wright, *An Autobiography*, p 169.

46 Dewey, op cit, p 213.

47 Hoffmann, op cit, p 92.

48 Hoffmann, op cit, p 92.

49 Hoffmann, op cit, p 92.

50 Connors, op cit, p 65.

51 Bachelard, *L'Expérience de l'espace dans la physique contemporaine,* quoted in Mary McAllester Jones, *Gaston Bachelard, Subversive Humanist*, Madison: University of Wisconsin Press, 1991, p 3.

52 Frank Lloyd Wright, *An American Architecture*, ed Edgar Kaufmann, Jr, New York: Horizon, 1955, p 61.

Chronology

1913
Kaufmann's Department Store leases Bear Run property.

1933
Edgar and Lillian Kaufmann assume ownership of Bear Run property.

October 1934
Edgar Kaufmann, Jr joins Taliesin Fellowship.

November 1934
Wright visits Bear Run site.

September 1935
Wright makes design drawings as Kaufmann drives to Taliesin.

December 1935
Rock quarry opened on site, test wall construction begins.

March 1936
Final working drawings completed by Wright.

April 1936
Construction begins on bridge and main house.

August 1936
Concrete slab poured for main floor.

October 1937
Construction on main house completed.

October 1939
Construction completed on guest house, servants' quarters and garage.

October 1963
Fallingwater and 1,543 acres donated to the Western Pennsylvania Conservancy by Edgar Kaufmann, Jr.

1979
Visitor centre built on Fallingwater site; 70,000 visitors annually.

Statistics

Location
Bear Run (stream), between Mill Run and Ohiopyle, Pennsylvania.

Area
Area of site: 1,635 acres in 1933, 1,914 acres at largest, 1,543 acres in 1963.
Area of house: 2,885 square feet (enclosed), 2,445 square feet (terraces).

Cost
$75,000 for house (1937 rates).
$22,000 for later finishing and furnishing.
$50,000 for servants' quarters, garage and guest house (1939).

Credits

Client
Edgar and Lillian Kaufmann

Architect
Frank Lloyd Wright

Project Engineers (Wright)
Mendel Glickman and William Wesley Peters

Supervising Apprentices (Wright)
Bob Mosher and Edgar Tafel

Contractor
Walter J Hall

Current Owner
Western Pennsylvania Conservancy (see also Note 25)

Bibliography

Abercrombie, Stanley, 'When a House Becomes a Museum', *AIA Journal* LXX (August 1981), pp 54–57.

Ackerman, James, *The Villa: Form and Ideology of Country Houses*. Princeton University Press, Princeton, 1990.

Apostolo, Robert, 'The Origins of Fallingwater', *Frames, Porte and Finestre* No 41 (December 1992), p 64.

'Architecture and Setting: Fallingwater, Bear Run, Frank Lloyd Wright', *Toshi jutaku* (November 1985).

'Art: Frank Lloyd Wright', *Time* XXXI (17 January 1938), p 53. (Fallingwater drawing on cover behind Wright).

10 Twentieth Century Houses. Exhibition by John Miller, Arts Council of Great Britain, 1980, pp 16–17.

Blanc, Alan, 'Forty Years On: Fallingwater, Frank Lloyd Wright's Most Famous House', *Building Design* No. 399 (9 June 1978), p 24.

Bolon, C, Nelson, R, and **Seidel, L** (ed), *The Nature of Frank Lloyd Wright*. Chicago University Press, Chicago, 1988.

Brownell, Baker and **Wright, Frank Lloyd**, *Architecture and Modern Life*. Harper and Brothers, New York, 1937. (Construction photographs.)

Connors, Joseph, *The Robie House of Frank Lloyd Wright*. University of Chicago Press, Chicago, 1984.

Donohue, Judith, 'Fixing Fallingwater's Flaws', *Architecture* (November 1989), pp 99–101.

Engel, Martin, 'The Ambiguity of Frank Lloyd Wright: Fallingwater', *Charette* XLIV (April 1964), pp 17–18.

60

Fallingwater and Edgar Kaufmann, Jr, Proceedings, Temple Hoyne Buell Center for the Study of American Architecture, Columbia University, New York, 1986.

'Fallingwater Saved Before It Is Imperiled: Kaufmann Makes Gift of House at Bear Run', *Architectural Record* CXXXIV (October 1963), p 24.

'Fallingwater, een landhuis van Frank Lloyd Wright', *Bouwkundig Weekblad Architectura* LIX (23 April 1938), pp 137–8.

'Fallingwater: Kaufmann House, Pennsylvania, Frank Lloyd Wright', *Kokusai Kentiku* XIV (April 1938), pp 149–56.

'"Fallingwater", vivenda en Pensilvania, arq. Frank Lloyd Wright', *Neustra Arquitectura* (October 1938), pp 336–45.

Frampton, Kenneth, '1936: Frank Lloyd Wright: Fallingwater, Bear Run, Pennsylvania, USA', *Modern Architecture, 1851–1945*. Rizzoli, New York, 1981, pp 398–399.

Frank Lloyd Wright's Fallingwater. Western Pennsylvania Conservancy, Pittsburg, 1988.

'Fallingwater, Bear Run, Pennsylvania, 1935', *Architecture + Urbanism* (September 1989).

Futagawa, Yokio (ed) and **Pfeiffer, Bruce B**, *Frank Lloyd Wright Selected Houses 4: Fallingwater*. ADA Edita, Tokyo, 1990.

Futagawa, Yokio (ed) and **Pfeiffer, Bruce B**, *Frank Lloyd Wright, Monograph 1924–1936*. ADA Edita, Tokyo, 1985.

Futagawa, Yokio (photographer) and **Rudolph, Paul** (text), *Frank Lloyd Wright: Kaufmann House, 'Fallingwater', Bear Run, Pennsylvania, 1936*. ADA Edita, Tokyo, 1970.

Futagawa, Yokio (ed), *Houses by Frank Lloyd Wright 2*. ADA Edita, Tokyo, 1975.

Gill, Brendan, *Many Masks: A Life of Frank Lloyd Wright*. Putnam's, New York, 1987.

Gill, Brendan, 'Edgar Kaufmann, Jr: Secrets of Fallingwater', *Architectural Digest* (March 1990), pp 50–64.

Hamlin, Talbot, 'F L W – An Analysis', *Pencil Points* XIX (March 1938), pp 137–44.

Harrison, Robert P., 'Fallingwater', *Forests: The Shadow of Civilization*. Chicago University Press, Chicago, 1992, pp 232–237.

Hildebrandt, Grant, *The Wright Space: Pattern and Meaning in Frank Lloyd Wright's Houses*. University of Washington Press, Seattle, 1991.

Hill, John deKoven, 'The Poetry of Structure', *House Beautiful* XCVIII (November 1955), pp 246–7, 348–50.

Hitchcock, Henry-Russell, *In the Nature of Materials; 1887–1941, The Buildings of Frank Lloyd Wright*. Duell, Sloan and Pierce, New York, 1941.

Hoesli, Bernhard, 'Frank Lloyd Wright: Fallingwater', *Architecture + Urbanism* No 118 (July 1980), pp 155–66.

Hoffmann, Donald, *Frank Lloyd Wright's Fallingwater: The House and Its History*. Dover, New York, 1978, 1993 (new colour photography). (Most comprehensive and accurate history of design and construction).

'A House of Leaves: The Poetry of Fallingwater', *Charette* XLIV (April 1964), pp 13–16.

'The Impact of Genius: Fallingwater, 1936', *House Beautiful* (November 1986).

Izzo, Alberto and **Gubitosi, Camillo**, (ed), *Frank Lloyd Wright: Drawings, 1887–1959*. Centro Di, Firenze, 1981.

Johnson, Donald Leslie, *Frank Lloyd Wright versus America: The 1930s*. MIT Press, Cambridge, 1990.

Kaufmann, Jr, Edward, *9 Commentaries on Frank Lloyd Wright*. MIT Press, Cambridge, 1989.

Kaufmann, Jr, Edward, 'How Right was Wright', *House and Garden* (August 1986).

Kaufmann, Jr, Edward, 'The House on the Waterfall', *Writings on Wright*. H Allen Brooks, (ed), MIT Press, Cambridge, 1981, pp 69–72.

Kaufmann, Jr, Edward, *Fallingwater: A Frank Lloyd Wright Country House*. Abbeville Press, New York, 1986. (First hand account by son of owner, later a scholar on Wright).

Kaufmann, Jr, Edward, *Fallingwater*. Architectural Press, London, 1986.

Kaufmann, Jr, Edward, 'Frank Lloyd Wright's Fallingwater 25 Years After', *Architettura* VII (August 1962), pp 222–80.

Kaufmann, Jr, Edward, 'Fallingwater at 50', *Interior Design* (July 1986).

Laseau, Paul and **Tice, James**, *Frank Lloyd Wright: Between Principle and Form*. Van Nostrand Reinhold, New York, 1992.

Levine, Neil, 'Frank Lloyd Wright's Diagonal Planning', *In Search of Modern Architecture: A Tribute to Henry Russell Hitchcock*. MIT Press, Cambridge, 1982.

Lind, Carla, *The Wright Style: Recreating the Spirit of Frank Lloyd Wright*. Simon and Schuster, New York, 1992.

Louchheim, Aline Bernstein, 'Frank Lloyd Wright Talks of His Art', *New York Times Magazine* (October 4, 1953), p 27.

McCarter, Robert, (ed), *Frank Lloyd Wright: A Primer on Architectural Principles*. Princeton Architectural Press, New York, 1991.

McCarter, Robert, 'Woven Space, Anchored Place: The Houses of Frank Lloyd Wright, 1935–1959', *GA Houses* 43, 1994.

Mock, Elizabeth, (ed) and Goodwin, Philip, *Built in USA Since 1932*. Museum of Modern Art, New York, 1945.

Mumford, Lewis, 'The Skyline – At Home, Indoors and Out', *The New Yorker* XII (12 February 1938), p 31.

Museum of Modern Art, *A New House by Frank Lloyd Wright on Bear Run, Pennsylvania*. MOMA, New York, 1938.

'New Visitors' Center Completed at Fallingwater', *Frank Lloyd Wright Newsletter* IV, No.2, (1981), p 18.

'One Hundred Years of Significant Building, 9: Houses Since 1907', *Architectural Record* CXXI (February 1957), pp 199–206.

Patterson, Augusta Owen, 'Three Modern Houses, No. 3: Owner, Edgar Kaufmann, Pittsburgh; Architect, Frank Lloyd Wright', *Town and Country* XCIII (February 1938), pp 64–5, 104.

Peterson, Jay, 'Nature's Architect', *New Masses* XXVI (8 February 1938), pp 29–30.

Plummer, Henry, *The Potential House. Architecture + Urbanism*, Tokyo (September 1989), pp 128–39.

Purves, Alexander, 'This goodly frame, the Earth', *Perspecta* (1989), pp 178–201.

Putzel, Max, 'A House That Straddles a Waterfall', *St. Louis Post-Dispatch* Sunday Magazine (March 21, 1937), pp 1–7.

Riecken, Andrea, 'Cinqueta anos da Casa da Cascata, s'imbolo do modernismo americano', *Projecto* (July 1987), pp 74–8.

Sainz, Jorge, 'El sueño cristalizado: Fallingwater a gusto de todos', *A and V* (1987), pp 56–8.

Saltz, Jerry, 'I Could Live Here', *Arts Magazine* (March 1989), pp 23–4.

Scully, Vincent, *Frank Lloyd Wright*. George Braziller, New York, 1960.

Smith, Norris Kelly, *Frank Lloyd Wright, A Study in Architectural Content*. Prentice-Hall, Englewood Cliffs, NJ, 1979.

Sorkin, Michael, 'Fallingwater at Fifty', *Connoisseur* (August 1986).

Storrer, William, *The Architecture of Frank Lloyd Wright: A Complete Catalog*. MIT Press, Cambridge, 1974, 1978.

Tafel, Edgar, *Apprentice to Genius: Years with Frank Lloyd Wright*. Dover, New York, 1979, 1985.

'Wright's Masterpiece Preserved', *Interiors* CXXII (October 1963), p 12.

'Wright's Newest', *Art Digest* XII (1 February 1938), p 13.

Wright, Frank Lloyd, 'Frank Lloyd Wright', *Architectural Forum* LXVIII (January 1938), pp 36–47. (Issue written and designed by Wright).

Wright, Frank Lloyd, *In the Cause of Architecture*. F. Gutheim, (ed), reprint of *Architectural Record* essays. McGraw-Hill, New York, 1975.

Wright, Frank Lloyd, *Frank Lloyd Wright: On Architecture*. F. Gutheim (ed), Grosset and Dunlap, New York, 1941.

Wright, Frank Lloyd, *Drawings for a Living Architecture*. Horizon Press, New York, 1959.

Wright, Frank Lloyd, *Frank Lloyd Wright: Writings and Buildings*. Kaufmann, Jr, E and Raeburn, B (ed), Horizon Press, New York, 1960.

Wright, Frank Lloyd, *An Autobiography*. Duell, Sloan and Pierce, New York, 1943.

Zevi, Bruno and **Kaufmann, Edgar, Jr**, *La Casa sulla Cascata di F. Ll. Wright: Frank Lloyd Wright's Fallingwater*. ET/AS Kompass, Milano, 1963.

Zevi, Bruno, 'Il vaticinio del Riegl e la Casa sulla Cascata', *Architettura* VIII (August 1962), pp 218–21.